Winner of the 2020 Midwest Book Award for *Hitman-Baker-Casketmaker: Aftermath of an American's Clash with ICE*

Longlisted for Best Independent Book of 2021 by *Shelf Unbound*

PRAISE FOR KLECKO

"In Klecko's personal, powerful collection of poems, he grapples with his feelings on a variety of topics including baseball, family and the fallout of a U.S. Immigration and Customs Enforcement Audit."

Tim Carman, *Washington Post*

"Klecko's affection for his crew spill out onto the pages."

Lee Svitak Dean, *Star Tribune*

"Klecko has become an ambassador for both poetry and immigrant issues."

Nancy Weingartner, *Food Service News*

"People in the industry know that bakers tend to be a spiritual lot. One of our most philosophical has to be the St. Paul baker that goes by one name: Klecko. He's written for years about the industry and baking life for different publications, but his new work is very personal, and important."

Stephanie March, *Mpls. St. Paul Magazine*

"Klecko – a baker who writes poems. A friend with integrity. A loyal human being. An award-winning author. This is so fucking good."

David Fhima, world-renowned chef and restauranteur

"Energetic host of readings as well as writing, Klecko is one of his own biggest fans. As he puts it, 'This is the most important book about hospitality since Anthony Bourdain's *Kitchen Confidential*.'"

Mary Ann Grossmann, *St.Paul Pioneer Press*

A BAKEABLE FEAST

Troy
WASH The
Whites

Klecko

OTHER BOOKS BY KLECKO

Zelda's Bed

The Dead Fitzgeralds

3 a.m. Austin Texas

Lincolnland

Hitman-Baker-Casketmaker: Aftermath of an American's
Clash with ICE

Out for a Lark

The Bluebeard of Happiness

A Pox Upon Your Blessings

Houdini in St. Paul

My British Hindu Bible

Robert Bly and the Monk in His Cell

Mayor 4 Life

Brando Land

A BAKEABLE FEAST

BREAD. SEX. HONOR.

BY KLECKO

PARIS MORNING
PUBLICATIONS

Published in 2023 by Paris Morning Publications
www.parismorningpublications.com

Copyright © Paris Morning Publications

Published and reprinted in the United States of America
ISBN: 979-8-218-31052-3
Cover design by Audrey Campbell
www.ataudrey.com

A BAKEABLE FEAST

BY KLECKO

THIS BOOK IS DEDICATED TO THE BREAD JACKALS . . .
ONE TRIBE
ONE LOVE

BAKING MEMORY #1

Harold had pink skin, he hated heat
He took salt tablets, every summer
His girlfriend drove him to work
Due to his collection of DUIs
Harold took off his shirt
During break time, and stretched out
On a shaded portion of sidewalk
When he got up, he left behind
A soggy sweat angel
His girlfriend worked at a sauna
A place where she met Harold
While selling him entry-level love services
One session, the love ramped up
A baby was born, the family took a flat
On a quieter section of Lake Street
On days that the temperature surpassed 90
Harold could be heard on the phone
Telling, advising, I don't care what it takes
Sell anything on the menu, just earn enough
To get us a motel room with air conditioning

BAKING MEMORY #2

On the loading dock of the Saint Paul Hotel
Five chefs circled a bus tub
Four standing, one crouching, stirring the contents
Pasta, cake, coffee, wine and vegetables
I approached, shot a glance at the Executive Chef
Who smiled, greeted and informed me
Pavarotti spent the night
Our engineer had to build a makeshift kitchen
In Pavarotti's room
He insists on cooking, for friends and guests
We've all heard he has skills, so . . .
Then the Executive Chef looked down
Upon the one crouching
I asked . . .
He doesn't have to eat that, does he
To which the Executive Chef replied . . .
That's what Sous Chefs are for

BAKING MEMORY #3

Close to 40 years ago
I worked on West 7th
"Friends" of the IRA
Stopped by each payday
To accept contributions
Rumored to support the lads
Back on the island
With weaponry, for the cause
Most of the Irish bakers
Kicked in a ten-spot

BAKING MEMORY #4

She left the Rez to make money
Stripping in the Capital City
Time passed, perverts accumulated
Life became sketchy, so . . .
She decided to settle down
Follow a childhood dream
Baking pastries and such
Late in the evening, we smoked
In my '78 Malibu
Looking at stars through the windshield
Large enough to rival a movie screen
Within weeks, the dream was dashed
When she determined
Mastering pastry was more difficult
And far less profitable than disrobing
Long enough to let broken souls ogle
On a Tuesday night, my night off
She untied her apron
And discarded her entire uniform
Before performing a dance
That was talked about for years

BAKING MEMORY #5

From 13 to 60
I've been unemployed 20 days
Ten days before my second wedding
The IRS shut us down, for not paying taxes
The bakery was wrapped in yellow tape
I went to a neighbor to call Brutus
To get a ride somewhere
Moments passed, he pulled up, he said . . .
Since you lost your job, I quit mine
Want to go see "BRAVEHEART"
We saw "BRAVEHEART," at the Mall of America
The movie was great
On the way back, we talked about it
Until we didn't, in silence I considered
I liked "BRAVEHEART"
But I might have enjoyed it more
Had I been employed

BAKING MEMORY #6

Billy was an oven man
He was handsome, his wife was ugly
After work, we'd party at his house
Billy would get drunk
And call his wife Bigfoot
Billy was an oven man
He pushed racks all night
In and out of the proof box
While doing this, he often yelled . . .
Hail Satan
The crew didn't like this
They didn't need their karma
Bleaker than it already stood
Billy didn't care, he continued . . .
Hail Satan
Until the wheel fell off a rack
Fracturing his collarbone
While recovering, Bigfoot divorced him
A fate predictable, but sad all the same

BAKING MEMORY #7

Chattanooga got out of treatment
He lived in a van, his body was covered
With half-finished tattoos
His specialty was mixing cookies
He claimed he baked in 31 states
He lived in a van, where he ran a business
Printing custom T-shirts
His favorite one announced . . .
SOBER AS FUCK
Chattanooga didn't last long
Child support caught up to him
In addition to baking, this guy must have created
A baby in half of the states
The day he left, he mentioned . . .
He was moving in with a Somali woman
Because her beauty was her tolerance

BAKING MEMORY #8

She specialized in pastry
She came from a huge family
Most of them worked in hospitality
She lived in a huge house
Family meant everything to her
She also liked whiskey and parties
Every year she hosted a Christmas bash
That started on Friday, ending Sunday
So remaining tribe members
Could go to Mass
She invited me to the annual kickoff
I dislike such events, but I went
I knew it was important to her
The living room had a showcase
Containing 50 nutcrackers
I mentioned, it must be hell to set up
She said she never took them down
I considered . . .
Staring at nutcrackers all summer
The thought made me nervous
An awkward thought, eventually erased
By several shots of Jameson

BAKING MEMORY #9

It came as a shock
When the pastry chef gave notice
To pursue a stint, on an island
Off of France, to work with a goat farmer
Doing God knows what
In addition to separating from her crew
She left behind a husband and two kids
To work for a goat farmer
On an island where she ended up
Doing almost nothing she wanted to do
The farmhouse was small
She slept in a loft, shared . . .
With the goat farmer's son, Sinbad
Who was reported to be obnoxious
In the depth of puberty, speaking broken English
While employing sporadic eye rolls, at a level
That can only be achieved by the French
In less than several weeks
She swiped a boat, and Sinbad's hat
Rowing by moonlight, to the mainland
By the end of the summer, she quipped . . .
Next year, I might consider China

BAKING MEMORY #10

Kevin the liar wasn't obese, his clothes were too small
Like Herman Munster or Porky Pig
His eyewear was ill fitting, squishing his face
It was hard to take him seriously, especially when he lied
Kevin did this and that, everything you'd expect
When in the presence of a millionaire
Which is what he claimed to be, the crew didn't care
They rolled with it, entertained
But it chapped my ass, just because
He spoke of beautiful escorts, art collections, security
    systems
Multiple homes, and of course, the schooner
Midweek, 4 a.m., I peddled toward home, drunk
Until I saw Kevin in a Laundromat
I had him trapped and dropped my bike to the curb
And waited, he didn't talk, I didn't talk
I just stared into his little beady eyes
I didn't even smirk, instead I held him hostage
With an ocular grip, when the point was proved
I stayed another five minutes, just because
The satisfaction this brought me, became testament
To what a tool I had become

BAKING MEMORY #11

The first time I became supervisor
The first guy I disciplined was Tommy Trutt
Tommy ran the bread divider
Panning super velvet white loaves
Trutt was tall, outweighed me by 80 pounds
He liked to smoke weed in his van on break
Breaks were 15 minutes, he took 30
I wrote him up, he took exception
Lifting me off the ground with one hand
Clutching my throat, cutting off my airway
Just when I began passing out
He slammed me against the proof box
Before dropping me to the floor
Somebody tracked down the plant manager
Who asked what happened
When I said I slipped
The manager winked before walking away
Leaving me alone with Trutt
Who brought me to his locker
Where he gave me one of his Burger King Whoppers
And an open-ended invitation to join him anytime
In his van, where he would get me high

BAKING MEMORY #12

I wasn't supposed to be there, it was Tuesday, my day off
But for reasons I don't remember, I was there
Playing witness to the accident
No one can be certain if he was stoned
But Marco was known to hit the hookah on break
And he had just come off of break
As I scaled 200#s of pan breads
Marco switched the pressure plate
On the bread molder, while it was running
His middle finger got caught in the drive chain
The machine seized, until it continued
Marco's finger fell to the floor, amidst blood spray
The amputation wasn't clean, the end of his finger
That tore away from the hand was jagged
People screamed, Marco wasn't fazed
He wasn't frightened, he looked annoyed
Ownership was angry when we called an ambulance
Insisting a crew member should have taken him
Marco received $8000 for his trouble
Ownership didn't want this amount revealed
Insisting it could tempt others
To intentionally part with their digits

BAKING MEMORY #13

Nick Q was released from prison
And relocated to St. Paul, because . . .
He claimed he had a brother
Who built champion caliber dragsters
The crew and I never met Nick Q's family
But sometimes we met his dogs
He was a volunteer dog walker
For the Humane Society
But, eventually he gave up that position
When asked why, he explained
On Easter morning he walked a pit-bull mix
They stopped to rest on a hill
The sun was shining, they stretched out
Nick closed his eyes while holding the leash
The pit-bull was large and laid on Nick
And proceeded to hump his thigh
The weight was too much, Nick was pinned
Until the pit-bull had satisfaction
When the crew heard this, we roared
Until we realized, Nick wasn't laughing
Then we felt bad, realizing
Pit-bull love isn't a joking matter

BAKING MEMORY #14

He came from India to Minnesota
But he was involved with computers
This was his path
He missed his country, he missed his family
And started an affair with the bottle
It knocked him off his course
Sending him to us, at the bakery
Ananda was kind, gentle, deliberate in tone
But, he couldn't find fifth gear
He couldn't meet production's required pace
On a day he and I weren't at our best
I called him out, in front of the crew
He turned and snapped at me
The bakers recoiled in dismay
Silence filled space, all eyes turned on me
To witness my reaction
Which was . . . Get the fuck out
Ananda approached me and bowed
He apologized and asked for pardon
I withheld it and sent him away
A decision that failed Ananda
As well as myself

BAKING MEMORY #15

She wanted Italian, they were booked
She was sad, I walked outside
Looked for a door next to a dumpster
I pounded three times
Hard
A woman in a chef coat answered
I told her I was in hospitality
I told her I was from out of town
I told her I didn't have reservations
But I had a wad of cash
And I would be happy to bribe
The woman chef smiled
The lobster ravioli was divine

BAKING MEMORY #16

Grap wore bandanas
Played harmonica in his pickup
He only knew one song
"Oh, My Darling Clementine"
On his bicep, he had a tattoo
Of a swastika, and font which read
Harley Davidson
However, the "I" in Davidson was omitted
Forgotten by the tattoo artist
When I addressed this to Grap
He chuckled, explaining . . .
The joke was on him
I traded the guy a full bottle of speed
For the tattoo
He never knew, I pinched half the bottle

BAKING MEMORY #17

Thurman Perk looked like
Howdy Doody or Opie Taylor
Pumpkin hair, layered freckles
Mornings he attended college
Designed for Pentecostals who wanted to preach
Minnesota was far away, from South Carolina
From his wife, who was about to celebrate a birthday
Perk had a passion for serving God
Perhaps this calling
Deluded his romantic sensibilities
He knew it, so he asked the crew . . .
What should I send my wife
It needs to be something special
Something romantic, ideas were submitted
Most of which were sincere, many of them logical
Tick – Tock, days passed until the pastry chef asked . . .
What did you get her
Perk straightened up, before disclosing . . .
A pill box
The pastry chef slackened and glared
While reminding all in attendance . . .
God hates stupid husbands

BAKING MEMORY #18

Sebastian Gold looked like . . .
Luca Brasi from "THE GODFATHER"
If Luca Brasi wore pink hoodies
And stretched his earlobes
With fluorescent gauges
Sebastian wore kilts to work
Or metallic pants made of satin
The day before Sebastian went to treatment
He showed me a picture of his prized collection
41 Raggedy Ann dolls
The day after Sebastian returned from treatment
I told him, I missed him, I loved him
And was proud of his recovery efforts
Words powerful enough to move my friend
Past his comfort zone, as illustrated when
He wrapped his arms around me, placing me . . .
In the midst of a gigantic bear hug

BAKING MEMORY #19

Terrence was kind and queer
He lived at the mission
He was fragile and undernourished
His dream was to buy a car
Move to Minneapolis
Work downtown at a hotel
He asked for a job, I only had an oven slot
A position that required strength and stamina
I worried the jackals on bread crew
Might eat him alive with homophobic antics
To my surprise, the jackals fed Terrence
Every day, restoring him to fit form
It took eight months, but Terrence finally got his car
And prospects for work across the river
At the end of his final shift
The jackals lined up to issue their farewells
As Terrence extended his arm to shake hands
The crew refused
Opting to mob him with hugs

BAKING MEMORY #20

Thomas O'Morda liked me
Because I was Irish
Hated me when I drank vodka
Claiming such acts placed me
Beneath Protestants
His Thermos was filled with Jameson
He never appeared drunk, just crazy
In the break room he drank instead of eating
He enjoyed People magazine
He turned to pictures of celebrities
And licked their faces
On a night of below zero temps
He asked for a ride, I was afraid to say no
When I pulled up to his place
He said he wanted to grab me a book
Minutes later, he ran out of his house naked
Making his way to the street, where he howled
I drove away, and never spoke of the incident

BAKING MEMORY #21

Cooch lived on the Eastside
In a house that looked like Herman Munster's
He had no money, he had no hope
He sported a tattoo that read . . .
BORN TO LOSE
His ex-wife was hot, past his pay grade
He paid her astronomical child support
He grew weary, he grew gaunt
Several days a week, he couldn't afford to eat
Bread crew jackals threw potato chips
Onto the production floor
Placing bets on when their helpless coworker
Would bend over and sustain himself
By eating their debris

BAKING MEMORY #22

Ronald Welder was the late night dishwasher
He was big, had a lazy eye
Cut his own hair without the benefit of a mirror
It was difficult to discern
If he was special or genius
He often wore the same gray "white" T-shirt
But he smelled good, like Irish Spring soap
Ronald Welder displayed a demeanor
Between Rain Man and Jeffrey Dahmer
Sometimes cops would stop by
And speak to Ronald in privacy
At the conversation's conclusion
They handed our dishwasher cans of Sprite
Ronald Welder loved Sprite
So much so, if you touched his can
He growled in a ghastly tone
Ronald Welder was hard to read
Possessing a "freak out factor"
Clear enough to make the bread jackals realize
It was more than bad form
To disturb his soda

BAKING MEMORY #23

Sunday mornings, Rico brought his daughter to work
She sat on the production bench, kicking her legs
Back and forth, back and forth
Listening to Mexican radio, Rico disliked American radio
Except he liked the Cranberries, in particular, the song
    "Dreams"
At the end of the song
He sang along with Dolores O'Riordan
Those Celtic scat-lines
Aah, la – ah la-ah La la la
Aah la – ah la – ah Le la
One morning Rico pissed in shrubs
At the bus stop, cops saw this
And arrested him for indecent exposure
An easy target, a Mexican alone, he was innocent
Recently, I talked to a guy, who talked to a guy
Word is Rico is homeless
Begging for money, begging for drugs
Sometimes, I think of his daughter
Sitting on the production bench, kicking her legs
Back and forth, back and forth
I hope she's okay

BAKING MEMORY #24

Charlotte NC / National Baking Convention
On the first night, you look for vendors you know
To take you out for steaks and cocktails
On the second night, you hit the clubs
With friends and colleagues who faded from routine
On the final night, sit at your hotel's bar
Chit and Chat with whoever shows
That's what I did when the Yankees were playing the Angels
We cheered, we hissed, the entire room was drunk
When I noticed my bar tab was $140
I recoiled, I winced, I was disappointed with myself
Until I stood and announced with authority
The tradition must continue
Who wants the honor of paying Klecko's bar tab
Arthur from Atlanta slid the barkeep his credit card
The following day, when I sobered up
I was mortified by my conduct
Would I ever be able to look Arthur in the eyes again
NOTE TO SELF – Stay out of Georgia

BAKING MEMORY #25

All I ever wanted was to serve
John Paul 2, the Polish Pope
I wanted to bake at the Vatican
I wasn't afraid to share my vision
I prayed to Mary, and the Saints of Warsaw
I got a Saint Faustina tattoo
One day a letter came addressed to me
Sent from the Archdiocese
Everyone was excited
And wanted me to get my wish
For three days I carried that letter
Fasting and praying for deliverance
In a quiet space, I tore open the envelope
It was a letter from Archbishop Flynn
He said he bought my sourdough
He said it was divine
He said he liked to bake bread
Then he told me God loved me
Tears pried their way from my eyes
I couldn't stop, I was honored, I was sad
I wanted to get to the Vatican
I wanted to serve the Polish Pope

BAKING MEMORY #26

Swear to God
I baked a Bundt cake on PBS
They picked me up in a minivan
Painted in the likeness of Big Bird
In haste, we headed back to the studio
Prior to our arrival
The producer urged me to be concise
On script, economic in language
Finally, the camera counted down
3-2-1 . . .
As the light flashed, and before the host spoke
It just kind of slipped out
Grandpa loves you, Madison Rose
Loves you the most
My comments surprised the crew
I wondered if I annoyed them
After brief reflection
I realized, it didn't matter
These people would forget me within the hour
But my granddaughter
She would remember that moment
The rest of her life

BAKING MEMORY #27

In a bakery
When your wife files for divorce
The dough mixer will tell you
He never liked the bitch
In a bakery
When your dad dies
The oven man grows hostile
Itemizing his father's drunken exploits
In a bakery
When your dog dies
The crew will mourn in silence
Knowing certain forms of suffering
Are sacred and require reverence

BAKING MEMORY #28

Her name was Candice
She worked with the bread jackals
She was pretty, divorced and lonely
Living in a trailer park in western Wisconsin
An evening with Candice had two requirements
You had to bring a bottle, and stay until sun up
One night I joined her, on the loading dock
We smoked in silence, until she sobbed
She stared downward, shaking as she confessed
The reason the bench foreman isn't here
I went to his apartment last night
And rode him so hard, he rolled over, dead
I didn't know what to do
Should I have called the cops
I didn't know how to respond, so I told the truth
If you tell the heat, you killed a guy
From riding him too hard
That would sound like bragging
I'd advise against that
Candice cracked a smile, and shooed me away
So she could enjoy another cigarette in privacy

BAKING MEMORY #29

What you learn working a trade show
With a Beauty Queen
Nothing beats winning Miss Minnesota USA
On your first attempt
Judges seem to prefer contestants
From small towns
When you win your state's competition
People you've never met, offer you
$10,000 of free dental work
Nothing is more demoralizing than losing
A nationally televised pageant to a woman
Named Shandi, who goes on to become
A sideline reporter for a CBS
Tournament blackjack series
If you wear your tiara through the Taco Bell drive-thru
Chances are you will get your burrito for free

BAKING MEMORY #30

What you learn working a trade show
Next to a Munchkin
At 18 he appeared with Mae West
While under contract with MGM
He went to school with
Judy Garland and Mickey Rooney
It was Garland who invited him onto the Oz set
He marched as a Munchkin soldier
And was the candy-striped fiddler
Who escorted Dorothy, down the yellow brick road
Toward the Emerald City
After retiring he worked for charities to raise money
For the St. Louis Police Department
This is where he met Cardinal slugger Mark McGwire
The two men became friends
When asked if calling him a Munchkin
Was politically incorrect, he responded . . .
You are what you are
And I am a Munchkin

BAKING MEMORY #31

A message was sent to me
From the United Arab Emirates
From a woman who was my interpreter
While I worked in the Siberian Arctic
Informing me that our bodyguard
From the diamond pits
Had recently been found dead
When I asked how he died
She remarked, such details are never given
When I asked if there was family
I could pass my sympathies to
I was told . . .
Protectors seldom have forwarding addresses

BAKING MEMORY #32

I was standing in front of the Kremlin
With Potato Girl
Sipping Cokes, exchanging notes
We were going to change the world
She wanted to bring Jesus
To the Motherland
Filling souls, instead of bowls
To leave an eternal brand
Empty stomachs and empty minds
Are quick to gather dust
Holy Bibles and prayer cards
Mean nothing without trust
So I made bread
Tangled up in red

BAKING MEMORY #33

She asked if we had any openings
For her son, I wasn't sure
So I said yes
The kid went by the name "Blue"
He was big and strong
Qualities not to be dismissed in a bakery
Halfway through the interview
My security service called
My house was being robbed
I terminated the interview without notice
I sprinted to my truck
Drove at menacing speeds
With hopes of catching the robbers
Out of nowhere
In the corner of my eye, sat Blue
In the shotgun seat, grinning
I mentioned the interview was over
Didn't he realize, I was being robbed
To which Blue responded . . .
Just so you know boss
I've always got your back

BAKING MEMORY #34

It isn't often I take time
To listen to the angels murmur
But sometimes I do
On one of these occasions
I overheard gossip suggesting
God made a mistake by outsourcing manna
For "The Last Supper"
This decision outraged the soon-to-be Messiah
Because he told the Almighty to order sourdough
The gaffe was averted
When the Saints of Warsaw prophesied
One of their own would be born
Into the arms of America
In addition to providing the finest baked loaves
He will design Heaven's eternal menu
When one passes through the pearly gates
Rules will no longer exist
However . . . it should be known
Those ordering meat during Lent
Will be seated with the Philistines
And the Lutherans

BAKING MEMORY #35

She told me . . . I thought of you recently
When I was in Rome
Gathering inspiration for a new menu
I was in my hotel room, feeling lonely
Until I heard a loud noise overhead
It sounded as if something
Was about to land on the roof
I became curious, and peeked through the curtains
To my surprise, I saw the Pope
Riding shotgun in a helicopter
When he noticed me, he waved
Later I was told
These flights are not uncommon
He enjoys praying for the Holy City from above
The whole event was so startling
Did I mention, I waved back
As he flew away
I wished you could have been there

BAKING MEMORY #36

The bakery owner was broke
In desperation he subleased our facility
To a woman, her husband was dying from cancer
Until she developed bread, reported to save his life
When we punched out, they punched in
Most of their staff was openly queer
Unusual in this time
Almost forbidden in this neighborhood
Two of their guys wore black chef coats
With pink pentagrams embroidered
Directly over their hearts
These guys gave off a "creep" vibe
Mullets hung off skulls attached to bodies
Between gaunt and emaciated
Our crew despised them
We didn't care who they slept with
Or who they prayed to, they were night crew
And if you've ever worked hospitality
You know for a fact
Everybody hates the night crew

BAKING MEMORY #37

The bakery's old
Hallways cold
Condensation
Causing mold
On the baseboards
On the wall
Clock strikes midnight
Ovens call
I'm going to rise tonight
Close your eyes tonight
Knead the world while you sleep
Pray to God your soul to keep
Bones are cold
Eyes are old
Seeing stories never told
Turn the deadbolt
Darkness crawls
Clock strikes midnight
Ovens call

BAKING MEMORY #38

On a Sunday morning sidewalk
In downtown Minneapolis, three vans pulled into
The gas station parking lot
Where our cracked-up delivery truck was towed
It was sunup, we were sweaty
Most were tired, we reminded me of Amish folk
Gathering from near and far, to raise a barn
Most were tired, we transferred donuts and cakes
Into our rides, knowing accounts were waiting
The clock was ticking, I drew the St. Paul route
Zoom- Zoom, I made my drop
People smiled, I figured the worst was behind me
But then I heard on the radio, Vida Blue died
Like Vida Blue, I am a lefty
My first glove was the Vida Blue model
When I pulled into the bakery parking lot
Geese hissed at me as I remembered
My uncle took me to Arlington, Texas
To watch Vida Blue pitch against Ferguson Jenkins
I must have been nine
This memory served as a reminder
How blessed my life has been

BAKING MEMORY #39

The break room wasn't dirty
Just unorganized and overrun
With Styrofoam and muffin cups
Surrounding John
Sitting at a table containing
No food or drink
In front of him, an envelope
It wasn't sealed, I looked at him
He nodded, so . . .
I picked up the envelope
I pulled out the card meant for his wife
It wasn't a Hallmark, it was homemade
Blotches of color, illegible scribbles
But the primary message
Was more than legible, it was beautiful
Stating . . .
In our next life, I will find you
And take you to a place that surrounds us
With the odor of elephants and rain

BAKING MEMORY #40

(1)
The first book I had published
Was "K-9 Nation Biscuit Book (Baking For Your Best Friend)"
A series of dog biscuit recipes
My first tour stop in support of the book
Was NYC, Martha Stewart Radio
That was my first trip to the Big Apple
I was excited, I was nervous
The night before I left, I went to the home
Of my writing coach "Big Vanilla"
After listening to the coastal antics of his youth
We drank three bottles of red
As I was about to leave, my friend hugged me
And handed me an envelope
He didn't mention what it contained
Or how valuable its contents were
I found out the following day
As I buckled up, and my jet taxied toward takeoff
This was an appropriate time
To open the envelope, and view its contents
A message of encouragement
The letter read . . .

(2)

When I was in LaGuardia it was 70 degrees
All I needed was a jacket, for three days I walked the streets
Leery of beggars who seem to know something
While shadowy figures lurked in the doorways
But the temperature began to fall
And the canyon gusts lifted plastic sacks, like ghostly luggage
I came into my own, I am more used to winter than them
It is my element
As I walked in the wind along 6th Avenue
Muggers and murderers parted
Melted from their purpose by sled dog eyes
Urgent and cheerful on a cold-cold night

(3)
All these years later
My memory of the Martha Stewart Show
My memory of NYC, have faded
But that letter from Big Vanilla
Is something I will always remember

BAKING MEMORY #41

I liked her, but wasn't sure how much
She asked me to bake a cake and bring it to her apartment
I did, the unit was barely furnished
The living room had a couch, coffee table and ashtray
She sat next to me on the couch at a distance that indicated
She liked me, but wasn't sure how much
I asked why I brought a cake, she explained . . .
Her mother was coming home from prison
I wasn't sure what to do, so I placed her hand in mine
Exerting an amount of pressure
Indicating potential romance was momentarily tabled
The gesture was appreciated, a smile traced her mouth
Her shoulders began to sink, both of us leaned back
Melting comfortably into the couch, the day crawled by
About the time of evening when you turn on your headlights
The doorknob turned, both of us stood
Her mother was home, she looked agitated
And stared at her daughter, and then the cake, before
    saying . . .
Memories have teeth that bite
And without instruction, both women went into another
    room
And shut the door, leaving me to wonder

BAKING MEMORY #42

The popular poet, the one with grit
Posted on Facebook, she was in the woods
Surrounded by shadows, hills, fallen leaves
In the distance she saw
A red structure with white words "Poop Barn"
The popular poet, the one with grit commented . . .
They should have called it "Shit Shack"
It scans better, has good consonants
It's just got a way better ring
I responded . . . Klecko votes "Poop"
It's classic, one of the first ten words spoken
By toddlers with strong mental health
I get the allure of "Shit Shack"
It's strong, sexy and makes one smirk
But is "Shit Shack" reliable, will it hold up
We have a saying in the baking industry
That applies to situations like this
Date the Brioche
Marry the Rye

BAKING MEMORY #43

Consistent with routine, I arrived home
Halfway between sunset and sunrise
The house was hot, I went outside
Sat on the top step and smoked a cig, a silent night
I puffed while thinking, quiet
Shouldn't be mistaken for stillness, not in this neighborhood
My neighbor's door opened, a woman stepped out
Consistent with routine, she sat on a concrete stoop
Dangled her legs and smoked a cig while providing
 a narrative
Meant for everyone, and no one in particular
The bottom of her face was swollen and bruised
I puffed and looked at her
She puffed and told me to mind my own business
I went inside, the house was hot, the following night at work
We had extra blueberry muffins, they were huge
Fist-sized, coated with sugar, I grabbed two and a carton
 of milk
To share with her, when we finished, she offered me a
 cigarette
It was menthol, I had my own, she wanted to be kind
As I lit up, she told me . . .
The best thing about miracles is that they even exist
But then she reminded me . . .
I would probably never see one if I stayed in this
 neighborhood

BAKING MEMORY #44

When midsummer construction began on Phalen Corridor
Homeless people were driven out from their established site
Some pitched tents, others parked cars
In the woods behind my bakery
It was hot the morning I met my new neighbors
Twelve men, half my age, stood next to the recycling
    dumpster
Asking for cardboard to make panhandling signs
The sun was blazing, the asphalt at melting point
Nodding yes, I dropped a piece of cardboard
Onto the parking lot, placed my hands on it
And rattled off 30 push-ups worthy of a Marine's approval
The twelve men became merry, and for the next ten minutes
They followed suit, bobbing up and down
All of us, huffing, puffing and sweating
Throughout the summer, parking lot push-ups became
    routine
Most of us assembled daily, without formality of invitation
Killing time with my neighbors was something
I looked forward to, but then the snow came
Camp broke unannounced, leaving me to wonder
If it was wrong to hope they would return

BAKING MEMORY #45

Because St. Paul is a sanctuary city
Cops leave Mexican motorists alone
As long as they stay in St. Paul proper
As my bakers complied, they got cocky
Testing boundaries, planning excursions
To neighboring suburbs, I gave each employee
A business card containing my name and phone number
And told them in no uncertain terms
If the heat pulls you over outside of the Capital City
They're going to take your car
So just indicate your English is poor
Have them call me, within a few weeks, sure enough
Ring – Ring, Hello Klecko, we have a kid named Welco
He doesn't speak English, we are impounding his vehicle
We don't have time to wait around
But we'll leave him on the off-ramp
Of 35E and Yankee Doodle Road
If you're willing to pick him up
When I picked up Welco, I pointed out
You'll never get that car back
He smiled and told me in broken English
Not bad, not bad, I will get more

BAKING MEMORY #46

Welco was one of the Mexican crew members
Several things were unusual about him
He wasn't related to anyone in town
An unusual circumstance for a Hispanic baker
He also shined a sketchy aura
Many of the Mexicans stayed away from him
Claiming he was crazy
I probably shouldn't say this
Because it doesn't mean anything
But I swear to God
Welco looked just like Gollum
In Peter Jackson's "The Hobbit"
On a Friday during a run of hot dog buns
Two ICE officers announced themselves
And asked for Welco who joined them
As they pulled up social media posts
Displaying Welco shooting AK 47s
And other automatic weapons, I'm not familiar with
Within weeks, Welco was returned to Mexico
Even though few of us liked him, we had to agree
He was a fine oven man, and would be hard to replace

BAKING MEMORY #47

The bread jackals dubbed her Squirrelhead
Because she always seemed to have a pair of nuts in
    her mouth
She bedded down with the dough mixer
His brother, the bench foreman and a dairy delivery guy
Some suspected, she did the bakery's owner
She was beautiful, clone to a Barbie doll
Her husband caught wind of these exploits
And sought revenge by slashing
Half a dozen tires on our bread trucks
One morning I rode a bicycle to work
That evening it rained, Squirrelhead noticed
And instructed me to hop into her car
She drove me home, mostly in silence
The rhythm of the windshield wipers
Reminded me of other types of rhythm
In front of my house, she turned off her car
And asked . . . Have you ever considered
How wonder just slows down time
I shook my head no, to which she responded
Of course not, you're too young
Then she sent me off with an innocent hug
Telling me not to keep my girlfriend waiting

BAKING MEMORY #48

Slits came to the bakery without experience
Without references, he worked like a dog
Always on time, but something about him was off
His hair, shoulder length, textured like straw
Face pockmarked, eyes never surpassed half open
Something about him was off
He lived with his grandmother, he had no friends
One night, after the shift ended
Several of us broke into the pastry cabinet
We drank rum and became drunk
The radio was playing "Silent Lucidity"
By Queensryche, Slits started playing air guitar
He raised his hands in the air yelling . . . Magic . . . Magic
Then he told us he knew a wizard
Who cast spells on him, spells that caused his pants to drop
So the wizard could . . .
Silence passed, nobody moved, nobody spoke
Until Slits began to cry, before issuing an apology
Nobody moved, nobody spoke
Until Grant the oven man hugged Slits
While assuring him . . . We got you baby, we cool

BAKING MEMORY #49

Chuckles' father owned the bakery
Chuckles' father crashed the bakery
Leaving me unemployed
Ten days before marrying my second wife
Chuckles moved deep into Wisconsin
It took five hours to drive to his house
We would drink for eight hours
At an Italian restaurant
It took five minutes to walk back to his house
Where we slept three hours
Before waking up and going to a café
Pancakes – Pancakes
Big as tractor tires
After a hug, after a wave
I stopped at a gas station
That employed a 17-year-old girl
Who stood at the counter
Listening to religious radio
Surrounded by whiskey bottles
And porno mags, that would eventually
Find their way into the townies' homes

BAKING MEMORY #50

It's the last oven load, no one's around
Shut off the proof box, blow the boiler down
Build memories, for a city that sleeps
In a couple of hours, I'll wake my best friend
And take her to Ramsey County OB-GYN
Anxious to see, when our package arrives
It's the last oven load, witness the mice
I've got no one to talk to, so I talk to Christ
Envisioning him, in his native attire
Nobody's listening, so I can speak loud
To a pallet of flour, that makes up a crowd
An ocean of people, if you need them to be
It's the last oven load, the bread's almost done
I look to the east, and notice the sun
Crawling like me, on a New Year's Day floor
Loneliness framed by equipment that drones
Isolation amplified by working alone
Trading in dreams, for some weekend plans
The job is the palm, your absence the spike
But after some Folgers, and one Lucky Strike
Open your eyes, I'll be staring at you

BAKING MEMORY #51

Knowing how I disliked Garrison Keillor

Without provocation

The pastry chef entered my office

Smirking, because she received

A second-hand invite to a gala

Taking place at his home

Taking place that very night

Steal his salt and pepper shakers, I demanded

We'll put them in the break room

My request offered no purpose

But the pastry chef called it genius

Promising to fulfill my bidding

The following morning

As I prepared to hear a detailed account

The pastry chef yawned

While handing me a package

With contents I'm not at liberty to discuss

BAKING MEMORY #52

The foreman was summoned to my office
When he arrived, I pointed out the window
Overlooking the production area, I pointed and asked . . .
Why is there a child on bread crew
The foreman smiled, that's Alacran
His paperwork is clean, I called bullshit
And ordered to send the kid packing
The foreman closed the door and asked
You know the new janitor, the old man from Salvador
I nodded yes, the kid's with him, they crossed together
They live with eight guys, bad men
They have no money, my family feeds them
Is that our problem, I asked
The foreman replied . . . We are trying to get them out
The old man is afraid to leave Alacran alone at night
Those bad guys will do bad things to that kid
I sat, he stood, I waited, he stared
Eventually the foreman declared . . .
I'm going to leave now
I'm guessing you'll want "all" of us
To return to work, I didn't disagree

BAKING MEMORY #53

The Russian Bear entered
His generals stood at attention
Rank and file
The Russian Bear spoke
With the same calm employed by Brando
During "APOCALYPSE NOW"
He emphasized urgency
By tossing a trash can in the air
Scattering donuts and cookies
Across the floor, before saying . . .
In five years, most of you will be here
But the rest of your crew, can't you see
They are carpetbaggers, they'll be gone
They don't care that they're wasting our money
Then he waved his paw in the direction
Of the scattered baked goods
Before closing with . . .
They steal your money
It's not a secret, so you better realize
There is no Wizard of Oz
There is no secret sauce

BAKING MEMORY #54

When the Republican National Convention
Came to the Capital City
Municipal workers constructed a holding pen
A huge cage attached to the police station
Just outside the window of our bakery
Over the course of a week
Lunchtime was met with anticipation
The bakers born in St. Paul
Constructed crude banners
Offering encouragement
To the howling protesters, pent up
While the Mexican-born bakers
Asked amongst themselves
What is there to protest
When you live in America

BAKING MEMORY #55

In view of current custom
We were petitioned to provide
Sourdough for the soiree downtown
Where our friend Tunde
Entered our city by way of Nigeria
And Detroit
To make a special appearance
At the Third Bird
Preparing goat head soup
His head hurt from Scotch and plum sake
His checking account coasted on fumes
He said it was time to revisit poetry and chanting
He said it was time to say yes to everything
He said it was time to embrace death
As long as it didn't last forever

BAKING MEMORY #56

When the bakery folds
I think I'll switch careers
And apply to be a guardian angel
I'll bet they start me off on the third shift
Hovering over headboards
Fulfilling my responsibilities in stillness
And should this solitude become daunting
I would simply regain focus
Issuing prayers, poems and dreams
Amidst moonlight and nightlights
And if I should grow weary
I would rock ever so slowly
Humming psalms of protection
To the squeaking of a hamster wheel
And when the daylight finally breaks
I'll probably wonder why I was needed
As I stare into the waking eyes
Of a child born so pure
There is no reason yet
To renounce evil

BAKING MEMORY #57

Angels flap their tired wings, hoping to create a breeze
Knowing there's no place hotter than a kitchen in July
They've been sent in several legions
To observe your every move
You don't believe in them, but your best friend does
You entered into my city
With a cloak and a beggar's purse
The appropriate credentials for a food service worker
Tonight I'm stuck in Moscow, watching CNN
The Pope's at Yankee Stadium, preparing his farewell Mass
I imagine blasphemous punch lines you'd deliver without
    effort
Then I feel nervous because I know they'd make me laugh
The Russian Chess Federation was closed when I stopped by
I bribed the guard and he let me look inside
I stared at empty tables where your heroes waged their wars
I told their ghosts that Bobby Joe would kick their ass
Montreal, Chicago, Minneapolis too
Your tank was almost empty
If you didn't leave soon, you'd never get back home
Angels clip their tired wings, they're not going anywhere
They prefer your company and reside in Kansas City

BAKING MEMORY #58

Johnny was the boss, I was his second
We made bread loaves for gas stations
Like Don Johnson, he had a gravel voice
Often times he declined to wear socks
Johnny had bar tabs past due
At every watering hole in Washington County
Often times his wife threatened divorce
We loved to drink screwdrivers
Shortly after sunrise, once our shift ended
We couldn't drink in our homes, both were occupied by wives
Glug – Glug we drank in the garage
A clean enough space, but clean and cold
After a while Johnny's wife wondered
Why we were doing so much garage time
Johnny mentioned we were building a dog house
The following day he brought home lumber
To enhance the ruse, he scattered it
Across the garage while explaining we needed to be on the
    same page
And even though I didn't have a dog, I should make one up
I chose a Corgi named Queenie
Johnny's wife eventually divorced him
An action which led to me becoming boss

BAKING MEMORY #59

(1)
Nicholas Maytag was in charge of the packing department
While he went to school, so he could move on to a fruitful
    future
He was smarter than the rest of us, but never condescending
He was stronger than the rest of us
But he couldn't fight worth a shit
When my girlfriend's empty parked car got slammed into
And pushed into the middle of the street
Nicholas Maytag returned it to the curb
By hand, with the assistance of the Cardenas brothers
Nicholas Maytag had a wealthy girlfriend
Who was beyond tall with striking features
On occasions when she dropped off lentil burgers
For her beau
She continued to find creative ways to let our crew know
She didn't like us, or approve of our position
In her future husband's life
Nicholas Maytag graduated college, got a job
And pursued a life of happiness
Just at a point when I forgot him
I ran into him at the St. Paul Farmers Market

(2)

I asked him about his job

He said . . . It's good

I asked if he married his girlfriend

Nicholas Maytag paused, eventually spilling the beans . . .

A couple months before we were going to get married

She went down to Florida with friends

She was only gone a week

While she was there, she tried smoking crack

She got hooked immediately

After she came home, she disappeared

We found out she was back in Florida smoking crack

She ran out of money, so she started sucking dick

Her parents found out and asked me to fly down there

At this point, I didn't want to marry her

I was kind of pissed that she destroyed our future

When I found her, she actually had a pimp

He didn't want me to talk to her

But I did, and she basically told me to fuck off

After thinking about it, I realized that was my only play

Think about it, who wants to marry a dick-sucking crack head

Not me

BAKING MEMORY #60

We called him Puma
He was raised in an Austrian family
He was raised in a bakery
He was good with pastry
He was divorced and lived with cats
He took time off to drive a tank
For the U.S. Army, along the Czech border
Then he came to us, he liked solitude
He hid in the freezer
One day while pulling cakes, he said . . .
I learned a new word "apricity"
Several months later, I went to Asheville
To visit the grave of Thomas Wolfe
At the cemetery
The snow had settled, the wind was cold
The sun . . . shining
It wasn't till that moment
I understood Puma's joy
Or the value of apricity

BAKING MEMORY #61

J – Smooth was kind
J – Smooth was quiet
Each time I called him after work
To discuss a work-related issue
He never picked up
One day I asked J – Smooth
Why don't you answer my calls
J – Smooth explained . . .
After work, I go home and do chores
I live on a farm
I do barn stuff
I asked . . .
Like milking cows
J – Smooth answered . . .
We don't have cows
But I have a lot of cats
I had no idea what that meant
So I leaned on my understanding
That not all trails need to be pursued

BAKING MEMORY #62

When the Archduke of Austria came
They sent 40 taste testers
20 from Austria, 20 from Hungary
When Gorbachev came they sent KGB
To sift through our flour bins
Looking for crushed glass
When Bush Sr. came
Two Secret Service taste testers
Criticized most of our wares
When Clinton came
He came alone
And said . . . Thank you
Before asking for seconds

BAKING MEMORY #63

(1)

The Morris sisters were entry level
Icing cakes, decorating cookies
When they found out I was headed to Nebraska
They insisted I stop at Joe's Café
Molly assured me their biscuits and gravy were epic
Mandy, on the other hand, mentioned . . .
The chicken fried steak was the bomb
What the Morris sisters neglected to tell me
Was that if I stopped at their favorite destination
Chances are that my experience would become regal

(2)

On the first day, Joe's Café

Hung a big screen TV on their wall

All the customers watched CNN

There was a special presentation

Of the Diamond Jubilee

Where the Queen floated down the Thames

On a royal barge, red & gold

1000 vessels floated past

14 miles of Union Jack bunting

And a belfry boat glided close behind

Mimicking Big Ben's ringtones

When our waitress returned

She became caught up in the fanfare

And placed her order pad on the table

While informing her customers . . .

We won't see that in Omaha

BAKING MEMORY #64

I was trying to drop off an order
Of hamburger buns, I took a wrong turn
I cut through the airport
I got to the place where you drop travelers off
I almost drove by, but then I saw an old man
Embracing a woman, who may have been his wife
Their moment of separation was touching
Touching enough to turn off the ignition
And watch other people separate from one another
On a sidewalk that offered departure
To each corner of the globe
If you stand in one place, engulfed in this mob
You will witness people exercising emotions
Ranging from despair to elation
I only stayed seven minutes
People are flawed – People are stupid
They disappoint
And seldom deserve trust
But if you stand outside an airport
When people send those they love away
It might be just enough to give you hope

BAKING MEMORY #65

Johnny Boy was self-proclaimed trailer trash
He explained there were three kinds of men
Mechanic Guy, Sports Guy and Hunter Man
Johnny Boy was a Hunter Man
On days off he could be found
On Grey Cloud Island
Spearing carp and drinking beer
Johnny Boy caught me in the break room
10:55 P.M., minutes before our shift started
Johnny confessed after yesterday's shift
He snorted lines of crank and played dice games
He hadn't been to sleep in 36 hours
He didn't know how he could make it
Through another shift
He asked me if I thought he should do another line
I said . . . Let Go and Let God
Johnny Boy laughed until he vanished
Into the locker room, where he did a fat line
20 minutes later, Johnny dropped in front of the ovens
An ambulance carted him away
I don't think he died, but I never saw him again

BAKING MEMORY #66

When I was young, Snuffy was old
He had long gray hair he combed into a "duck's ass"
He wore a motorcycle jacket
And listened to doo-wop
Just like greasers, he wore low-rider pants
That often exposed an upper third of his butt crack
One night the mixer distracted Snuffy
Wrestling with him playfully
While a guy from the donut belt
Used precision to slide a quarter into
That upper third of Snuffy's butt crack
Hours went by, bread jackals roared while ranting . . .
Who broke the jukebox
Hours went by, inching toward the shift's end
Before Snuffy discovered the source of our laughter
After he unwedged his ass, he became irate
Until he found Bobby-Uffda who was the same size
Snuffy turned purple and began wailing on Bobby-Uffda
Who couldn't stop laughing, instead he curled in a ball
And through the laugher, Bobby-Uffda kept repeating . . .
Who broke the jukebox

BAKING MEMORY #67

124 Degrees . . .
With two hours before sunrise
The last baker enters the break room
Joining a crew, soaked and faded
Their shift hasn't started
Condensation on the windows
Gatorade puddles serve as warning
This won't be a day for talking
In silence they wait
Listening to the compressors wheezing for air
On the other side of the oven room's door
Each considers leaving, but fears being the first
To turn tail while their brothers face the dragon
Only years later will they realize
Why they had to carry on
It wasn't for themselves
But each other

BAKING MEMORY #68

(1)

In the village along the river
Came low-cost housing
Locals rumbled, I baked bread
One of these new residents
Joined us at the bakery, his name was Dante
Originally from the Motor City
Dante fit in, showed up on time, pulled his weight
Without effort he became a natural crew member
One morning after work, me and the boys joined Dante
At his apartment, to drink rum, and be merry
Glug – Glug 151
Glug – Glug all was fine
Dante sat down to a small electric keyboard
Rattling off some Brahms or Beethoven
None of us was qualified to critique this sonata
But all of us were bright enough to understand
Dante had a gift

(2)

As I became drunk

I began to notice Dante had slender fingers

Contrasted by forearms like Popeye

I began to notice

The 122 family pictures scattered across the walls

Each containing men in Adidas track suits

Women in Baptist dresses

Numbness moved in, the music stopped

As Dante's wife appeared, displeased

She wanted money to get her wedding ring out of hock

The room fell silent, Dante said . . . Baby

His wife stepped out to the parking lot

All of us followed, Dante said . . . Baby

Until Baby spit on the pavement

An action that released demons from Dante's soul

Without warning, he charged and began slapping her

With a fury that sprang from an unseen space

The boys and I restrained him

Until the police arrived

That closed the book on Dante

BAKING MEMORY #69

(1)
Bang – Bang – Bang went the trolley
Somewhere within the historic district of Savannah
As our tour guide, Tammy with a "T"
Told us to keep an eye open for her lost Chihuahua
The trolley halted in front of a pub
Displaying a red telephone booth and a Union Jack
Tammy with a "T" announced . . .
This is where Julia Roberts (in one of her movies)
Walked up to that window, peeked in
And caught her fella cheating
Bang – Bang – Bang went the trolley
And just like that I craved fish and chips
So I hopped off, went in, and scanned a menu
That offered bangers and mash, pot roast, shepherd's pie
But no fish and chips

(2)

When the server arrived, I made them aware

I think there's a mistake

Fish and chips have been omitted from the menu

The server rolled their eyes, while explaining . . .

We don't serve fish and chips

We don't even have a fryer

In a moment of panic, in a moment of disbelief

I went slack jawed, which forced the server to continue . . .

There is no law that says an English pub must sell fish
    and chips

Being that I'm not well-versed in laws pertaining to
    British cuisine

I couldn't disagree, but I was angry

And continue to be angry, to this day

I really was in need of a fish hook-up

Clang – Clang – Clang went the trolley

Tammy with a "T" could be heard in the distance

As my bangers and mash arrived

I sure do hope she ended up finding that Chihuahua

An appropriate conclusion one might expect

While experiencing that unique magic

You can only find in Savannah

BAKING MEMORY #70

The Archdiocese rewarded her with a house
Best described as a brick cottage
And every night for many years
A baker passed by with his four dogs
On one particular evening
For no particular reason
The Nun poked her head out the window
And asked . . . Do you know why
You spend so much time with those hounds
The baker paused and wondered
Was this some kind of Nun trick question
She continued . . .
We are all the same, but we are also very different
I believe this is your natural way of praying
Then she came out of her house and hugged the baker
Who returned home, with gratitude in his heart

BAKING MEMORY #71

(1)

Like the Royal Navy
Each bag boy at the Golden Valley Super Valu
Was trained to thrive in multiple stations
The brightest and best looking were placed in the deli
Located by the entrance, with the understanding
First impressions were paramount
The average were divided, between Produce and Stock
Respectable appointments
Yet untethered from grocery glamour
Then there were the bag boys under constant reminder
They were lucky to even be on the payroll
These misfits were sent to the Bakery
I was a bag boy at Golden Valley Super Valu
Can you guess where they sent me

(2)

At 13, I worked all summer
P.M. shifts, five days a week
Sometimes rules were bent
And I was allowed to work past midnight
Several of the bakers were Dutch
All of them were stern
Usually at the witching hour
We'd go out back to the dumpsters
Where the old bucks let me join in
Smoking Lucky Strike cigarettes
Drinking Special Export beer
Conversation was seldom
We just smoked and drank
While staring at the stars
A routine that convinced me
Baking was the equivalent
Of being a modern-day pirate
And if that was the case
I wanted to spend the rest of my years
Sailing the sea

BAKING MEMORY #72

Songa was Hmong, Laotian and young
Coming to us through adventures and peril
On a dark night, in the dead of winter
We hand rolled 22 billion bread sticks
Of the many topics discussed, our evening's feature
    discussion
Revolved around his description
Of the flight from his native country
Songa said . . . My brother and I built a raft to cross the river
We launched at night, the river ran swift
Patrol boats patrolled, catching us in their spotlights
They opened fire, I rolled off into the water
Clutched the raft, it was difficult to hold on
Eventually I pulled myself up
My brother was gone, I haven't seen him since
I was placed in a refugee camp
For five years I applied for French citizenship
They wouldn't have me, I had to accept second best
And come to the United States, to which I responded . . .
Seriously, you picked Paris over America
Songa explained . . . My life meant more than ever
I wanted to honor my family by existing in a place of beauty

BAKING MEMORY #73

Ollie lived past the metro outskirts
On a property equipped with a pole barn
Converted to produce pastry
Ollie loved Jesus and talk radio
I never saw him defeated, except . . .
The time Aerosmith complained
Calling his blueberry pies amateur
We outsourced product from Ollie
He would bake pastry
Then deliver it in the middle of the night
On one such delivery, he was on the freeway
In the dark, he heard . . . "THUD"
He struck a man and killed him
Dismayed and confused, Ollie pulled over
Into a Walmart parking lot
He called the police and informed them of the incident
Confessing he unintentionally wasted a man
The woman on the police line
Chuckled against better judgement, and informed
A unit is in route, but don't worry
You're the third person to hit that body and call
I'll bet it was the first car that killed the victim

BAKING MEMORY #74

Production takes place
In a part of the city
Where beauty can take no root
Cinder block borders
Turn back confident musings
Squelching all hopes of escape
Yet, there she sits
Alone in the break room
Next to the Coke machine
And it's that very moment
His fortune whispers
This is the place to be

BAKING MEMORY #75

When a man, six foot three, 250 pounds
Walks toward the bakery
Most people coming from the opposite direction
Look down at the sidewalk
And issue a nervous salutation before passing
When a man six foot three, 250 pounds
Covered with tattoos
Walks toward the bakery
It's common for those approaching
To cross the street, they pass on the other side
When a man six foot three, 250 pounds
Covered with tattoos and a shaved head
Walks toward the bakery
With a Chihuahua named Frito
Most pedestrians freeze, not knowing how to proceed
When a man six foot three, 250 pounds
Covered with tattoos and a shaved head
And combat boots walks toward the bakery
Carrying a Chihuahua named Frito
Carried in a plaid puppy purse
Everyone retreats at an accelerated clip
Everyone, without exception

BAKING MEMORY #76

Anna tended bar at the Glockenspiel
Sometimes, after I dropped off loaves of rye
She would wink, and float me a Pilsner
One day, coincidentally
I ran into her in Minneapolis
At a tattoo parlor, where she sat in silence
Empty eyes, never flinching
While the tattoo artist
Did a cover up on her tramp-stamp
The original tattoo was the name
Of a former lover
Of the father of her daughter
Of the guy who put a bullet
Through her ribcage
Some memories fade, Anna explained
But this Mother Fucker
Is getting covered with roses
I don't want the bastard to vanish
I want him buried
Forever

BAKING MEMORY #77

Along the Black Sea
Most of us drank too much
Our shift started early
At 3 a.m. we arrived at the bakery
In silence we entered a windowless building
Under a cloak of darkness
All thoughts were isolated
Our boredom seemed independent
Because each of us thought
Our drudgery was exclusive
Finally, there was a murmur
Forcing everyone to give attention
To a spectacle
Through the keyhole to the entrance
Streamed a razor of light
Enough to fill a pocket of sunshine
And give our dark day meaning

BAKING MEMORY #78

When the shift is over
There's nothing creepier than walking home
Hours after sundown
Hours before sunup
With the wisdom of your elders echoing in your mind
Don't go out after midnight
Nothing good can happen
Safety is accompanied by sunshine
Perverts, addicts and thugs
Close their shops of chaos
At or around 3:30
When their plunder has disappeared
Between this moment and sunrise
Sanity is briefly restored to the world

BAKING MEMORY #79

In the last 36 hours
I got hit, heavy with the flu
My wife broke her elbow
I hit a deer, head on
(Hwy 61 – north of Johnson HS)
Car is totaled, deer is totaled
Wife's surgery was cancelled
The surgeon called in
I must say, it's been stressful
But a car can be replaced, bones mend
Flu will eventually disappear
But, it's got me thinking how fortunate I am
Many people suffer worse, I forget that
But, it's good to remember
It's good to remember what you forget
Thanks to the bread jackals
For covering for me

BAKING MEMORY #80

I have it on good authority
After a baker passes middle age
But he hasn't quite reached old
A small window of time opens
And his sleeping pattern
Will return to its infant cycle
Where every hour, on the hour
He awakes and is visited
By ghosts from the past
Who enjoy nothing more
Than illuminating moments
That everyone else has forgotten
If the memory is tragic
His wife cannot help
Because in the dark
When he hears her breath
Soft and rhythmic
The universe makes it apparent
He is on his own

BAKING MEMORY #81

Fat Randy only worked the bench
Never the ovens or mixers
He taught me how to handle dough
How to roll tight boules
He owned muscle cars and motorcycles
Lived in a trailer park, had a blonde pencil mustache
And a mullet perm, Fat Randy had clusters of skin tags
Hanging from his armpits
Swaying like dream-catchers on wind
He was known to let his awkward cousin
"Fat Ronnie" borrow his wife in return for cocaine
Fat Randy made it a point
Made sure I never had to walk home
He constantly gave me rides
Even though it was out of his way
Eventually he got caught selling "stuff"
And received 25 years
Fat Randy displayed affable gestures
Intended to lean on kindness
Fat Randy is better than he appears on paper

BAKING MEMORY #82

I still see her lips
Moving in slow motion
Forming promises of love
But I have to believe
She was uncertain of her feelings
Since once a year, for several years
She gave me birthday treats
Purchased at the grocery
Or perhaps a high-end gas station
When I flipped the lid open
The cupcakes were always frosted
Chocolate and vanilla
Candied confetti
Exploded in rainbow colors
Sweet shards of shrapnel
Scattered across the parchment
But the part I remember most
Were those scary plastic clown heads
Periscoping through the frosting
While grinning at my discomfort

BAKING MEMORY #83

(1)
In 2006, my past caught up to me
I was paid a visit, by a man in a trench coat
He mentioned it would be in all parties' best interests
If I helped the government
By running a series of scopes
To isolated places, sequestered spaces
I was assured the results would offer solace
Days passed, a Fed Ex envelope arrived
A series of e-mails arrived, and just like that . . .
I was headed to Siberia
Diamond City, the Asiatic Arctic
Listed below is an account
Of how the journey started out
It is also indicative of my entire tenure
With the United States government

(2)

I am flying commercial, six foot three, 262 pounds
Wedged between four Dutch boys
Watching "THE LITTLE MERMAID" in unison
A lanky American
Who looks like Abe Lincoln without the beard
Drops into the chair in front of me
Heading to Amsterdam with a choir
With a voice I'm guessing was falsetto
He announced his wife couldn't make it
She was scheduled as the tour's flautist
But her right hand was afflicted with drop palsy
Honest Abe reclines
Thus placing the back of his chair
Flush against my cramped thighs
Leaning forward, I flash him the "guy look"
Which, is just another way of asking
Do you really need to be such an A-hole
His silence indicated that he did
Maybe I was trapped with the guy's head in my lap
At least I wasn't a flautist with drop palsy
Constantly subjected to this lout

BAKING MEMORY #84

Tony O was too smart to be a baker
He could have been a rocket scientist
But he chose to bake
Tony O was an activist
He supported PETA
We worked in a rough neighborhood
Dog fights were a thing
Many of these dogs were tied to trees
Or locked in outdoor kennels
After loading the evening's final oven load
Tony O set the timer
For 40 minutes, and said with a smirk
Before that timer goes "DING"
Another dog will be liberated
Over the course of the summer
He set three dogs free
His tally almost reached four
But an anxious pitbull bit his hand
There was blood, pain and enough nerve damage
To prohibit Tony O
From unloading any more ovens

BAKING MEMORY #85

Top Chef has always impressed me
I forget if he's French or Moroccan
His children have bloodlines to Christians and Jews
Once I asked, which faith they were raised in
Top Chef replied . . . Whichever suits them
Although at one point he was touted
As a Los Angeles super chef
What people don't know
He's a better baker than cook
In L.A. he was employed by the Lakers
Now in Minnesota, among other things
All things cuisine with the Timberwolves
Go through him
One morning, downtown, I visited him
The restaurant was closed, we sat in the kitchen
Alone
Quiet kitchens are rare, I enjoyed this
Top Chef broke the silence
With what has become my favorite quote . . .
Restaurants are difficult
Bakeries are impossible

BAKING MEMORY #86

(1)
It was December
On the 400 block of Summit Ave.
I was prepared, but nervous
I was more than invited
I was commissioned
By the niece of Eugene McCarthy
Who doubled as an ex-wife
To Peter
From Peter, Paul and Mary
The event was to honor
The Duchess
Also known as the Capital City's Poet Laureate
In addition to serving lemon cake
I was asked to write and perform
An original poem
Here's what I came up with . . .

(2)

Nobody understands
The thought process of a woman
On the anniversary of her birth
Quite like the village baker
For he has set 1000 cakes
Before the fairer species
And he has deduced
What the majority will miss
The woman is not thinking about
The arc of her life
The losses she has suffered
Or how many candles are blazing
She's not imagining the perfect partner
She simply wants dessert

BAKING MEMORY #87

(1)
Recently I read, for 30 years
Kim Kardashian has looked at herself
In a mirror, 2 1/2 hours each day
Do the math, that's 27,375 hours
I wonder what she thinks
Primping, plucking, painting
I wonder what she thinks
What has she taken away
From this sizeable investment
Something profitable, I'm certain

(2)

For 30 years, Klecko looked into an oven

9 hours a day, looking at loaves

Do the math, that's 70,200 hours

What did he learn

If you're doing hospitality right

It stands opposed to vanity

There's nothing wrong with having fun

While feeding a community

But the second a baker steps out of humanity

The bread begins to lose its flavor

BAKING MEMORY #88

I worked the P.M. shift
When I came home, I drank wine
Red was a beverage foreign
To my nightcap rotation
I drank wine and watched a video
"THE LAST TEMPTATION OF CHRIST"
I became drunk and marveled
What a cast . . .
Harvey Keitel as Judas
Harry Dean Stanton as the Apostle Paul
David Bowie as Pontius Pilate
And Willem Dafoe played Christ
The following night, in front of the oven
I stood alone, considering Christ
I was sober as I pondered
As it occurred to me
Was it Christ who intrigued me
Or the performance of Willem Dafoe

BAKING MEMORY #89

The National Honey Board invited me
To a conference in Chicago
They never mentioned a limo
Would pick me up at O'Hare
I was dressed in designer sweats
Looking like a Russian Oligarch
Minus the gold ropes and hand guns
Circumstances caused me to laugh
Out loud, I seldom laugh
Especially out loud
During the commute, I posed
For dramatic selfies of . . .
Serious me, pensive me
Pragmatic me, and of course
Petulant me
Hours later, I wasn't surprised
To find nobody responded to my posts

BAKING MEMORY #90

When the conference was over
I waited for the limo to pick me up
And shuttle me back to O'Hare
To my surprise, a custom bus pulled up
I was forced to board the unusual vehicle
With eight fat guys
All of which were bakers
In quiet we got accustomed to our surroundings
Disco ball, strobe lights, thumping music, and of course
A stripper's pole placed in the middle of the walkway
Nobody spoke, a final baker boarded
A woman, young and fit
Before she had time to process
The driver engaged the ignition
Dance music blared
Amorous activities appeared on a jumbotron
Tension escalated at the speed of light
Until the driver hit the kill switch
And the bus returned to quiet
Until our female colleague confessed
I didn't like where that was heading

BAKING MEMORY #91

(1)
I think we talked about
The Martha Stewart gig
In an earlier installment
I think I thought
I was on the threshold
And about to be discovered
Possibly famous
Funny, years have passed
Many years, now that it's over
When I think about New York
I never think about the brief media blitz
Something far more rewarding occurred
45 minutes in Central Park

(2)

Between the hours of 3 and 4
Sat a man who was coming apart
A man at the end of some battle
Big drops of rain began to fall
Rain drops by the tablespoon
The man refused to move
A woman with a terrier
Stopped as if she knew him
Offering dry escort
Underneath her umbrella
The man began to cry
Who determines luck
Who makes up the rules
Why is value attached
To everything but me
The woman sat by his side
Put her arm around his shoulder
In silence the umbrella twirled
Until she offered explanation
Everything will be fine
Just not today

BAKING MEMORY #92

(1)
Originally they came from Romania
Or maybe Yugoslavia, for reasons never explained
Set base in Chicago, once a year, usually in spring
They made their way to St. Paul
Stopping at bakeries, unannounced, without invitation
Offering to fix our mixing bowls
At an unbelievable price
The bakery owner hashed out terms
With a guy named Luca
Their process lacked provisions or haggling
After shaking hands, the doors of Luca's van opened
Allowing tinsmiths to spill out
Executing their craft at makeshift work stations
Set up across the parking lot
Behind the bakery

(2)
We were instructed not to mingle with the tinsmiths
For reasons never explained
However, I broke protocol, unintentionally
When I went out back to smoke
Luca joined me, small talk began
I asked what he did for fun in St. Paul
He said . . .
He went to Minneapolis
To Lake Harriet
To paint the rose garden, then he asked
If I wanted to join them, I declined
How many times over the years
Have I regretted that decision

BAKING MEMORY #93

It is my understanding, almost nobody
Gets into baking to be a baker
More often than not, these positions are filled
By people who realized
They weren't bright enough
Diligent or wealthy enough to attend college
It is my understanding, almost nobody
Gets into baking, hoping to make it a career
For most, it's a pit-stop which serves
As a springboard memory, reminding them
There was that season
When they were lonely and unloved
It is my understanding, almost nobody
Gets into baking to be a baker
But on those rare occasions
When two intentional bakers meet
I'll bet you a dollar to a donut
Both parties will look at each other
Wondering . . .
What the fuck were you thinking

BAKING MEMORY #94

Chefs follow trends
Bakers follow science
Chefs – man buns
Bakers – crew cuts
Best chefs are coastal
Best bakers, in flyover country
Chefs dream of becoming celebrities
Bakers dream of vampires' flights
Chefs wear clogs
Bakers wear Red Wing boots
Chefs run from ghosts
Bakers run toward God

BAKING MEMORY #95

Wilson worked pest control
Surfacing at the bakery
The first Tuesday of each month
He was smart, but also scary
No matter what conversation topic
Trolled across our morning
He always inserted a rodent quip
We heard about rats in Utah
Rats in Jersey, not to mention
Rats in Chicago
The Chicago rats thrived in freezers
Like the freezer in the "ROCKY" movie
Where sides of beef hung
The Chicago rats climbed on top of each other
Creating a monolithic rat pyramid
Where the top rat would stand, gnaw
Across the top of the carcass, until
Gravity caused the beef to fall
Wilson was generous, constantly offering us Starbursts
But who's going to eat a Starburst
Touched by a guy who handles rats

BAKING MEMORY #96

One might suggest it was the result
Of growing up without a father
Others have offered, it's merely genetic disposition
Either way, I've come to terms with it
I lack mechanical aptitude
I'll never forget the time my grandfather
Stopped by my apartment
His eyes sparkled as he spotted
A Craftsman toolbox on my kitchen table
Like a child placed before a toy box
He opened it without permission
But just as the examination started
His enthusiasm waned
The contents were cake plungers
Fondant molds and pastry tips
He didn't seem to mind the brioche tins
Until I told him, they were "fluted"
Though the moment was awkward
I remained secure in my masculinity
But when he picked up my textbook
"Wilton's Course in Flowers and Cake Design"
What I wouldn't have given to find a place to hide

BAKING MEMORY #97

(1)
Friday, Saturday and Sunday
A soon-to-be defunct heavy metal radio station
Was going to play R.E.M.'s
"It's the End of the World as We Know It
(and I Feel Fine)"
In continuous loop, one supposes
The closing gesture was meant to offer
A defiant tone of gratitude
To their mostly cynical radio fan base
Connie K and I shared full weekend detail
Running the bread bench
Our bakery owner had recently died
Details hadn't been revealed, but he was young
Even though Connie K and I were at an age
Where personal problems should naturally eclipse
The aftermath of a fallen comrade
She said . . . There's nothing we can do for him
He's dead, but let's vow to leave the stereo
Turned to this station for the entire weekend
It will be our tribute to him
I pledged a vow and turned up the volume

(2)
On Sunday, through the afternoon
And into the night, Connie K and I
Went about our routine in quiet without conversation
The R.E.M. song surpassed redundant
I wanted to shut it off, but I couldn't
For an instant, I considered ending the tribute
To hell with the oath
But as I began processing this urge
Connie K broke into tears
I stood motionless, deadpan
Eventually she regained composure
She mentioned our dead boss
And how she fucked him for rent money
But now that he was dead
She'd have to move back with her ex-husband
So much for tribute, I turned off the stereo
And closed shop early

BAKING MEMORY #98

Across the river in Babylon
In the western suburbs
World Wide Headquarters
One of the biggest baking institutions
On the planet
Oceans of parking lot, immaculate lighting
Confidentiality contracts
New product ideations
Blue ribbon winners, Master bakers
Soundproof booths, when all is done
Down the hall, a pair of doors
18 feet high, cross the threshold
Enter the "Think Tank"
At conference tables made from exotic materials
Countless goons smirking
Winking, nudging, prodding for the best ideas
Pharisees will toss you 30 pieces of silver
But if you just cough up half-ass intel
It's still enough to send your son
To DC with his sophomore class

BAKING MEMORY #99

Dateline – Manhattan Kansas
Knowing this state offered minimal shade
Hot was beyond hot
The thermometer spoke of an abnormal register
Great time to take an artisan bread course
At American Institute of Baking
When I wasn't at class or the Last Chance Saloon
I rented a room at the Holiday Inn
Along with hundreds of evangelists
Attending a holy rollers' conference
Every ten feet some guy in a polyester suit
Did everything they could to save my soul
At night I smoked in the parking lot
Amidst God's servants, each of which
Blasted gospel hymns, Cadillacs and Lincolns
Open trunks, thumping subwoofers
A Baptist Preacher asked what I believed
I said . . . I don't know
The preacher put his hand on my shoulder and said . . .
Son, the only thing worse than an atheist
Is an agnostic baker, that doesn't even seem possible
I didn't disagree

BAKING MEMORY #100

(1)

Opera Lady was a friend of the family

About to celebrate her 50th birthday

She wanted to have a blowout, fine food, top shelf booze

And once everyone was buzzed

She'd take the stage at the Czech beer hall and sing operatic
ditties

Primarily to people who were clueless, unfamiliar with
fine arts

My job was to cater the event and help out at the bar

I pre-made much of the menu before the event

But the night before the party, I got thumped with the flu

A responsible person would have stayed home

But my involvement meant everything to Opera Lady

When in doubt, self- medicate, that's what I did

Rotating shots of TheraFlu and vodka

The following morning, I hopped in my truck

Realizing sometimes . . .

You just have to "Let Go and Let God"

(2)

Once my task was complete
I stepped into the beer hall bathroom
I kept my eyes shut, toweling off droplets
Running down my face, when I opened my eyes
There stood a woman
I thought I entered the wrong restroom
Until I noticed a urinal, my mind shuffled
Booze and bewilderment
Until clarity surfaced, this lady was transgender
My shock was apparent, reflected by her reaction
She was frozen in a flinch
I had caused this shame
How does one apologize
For involuntary actions
Having no solution
I placed my hand on her shoulder
Letting several moments pass in silence
Before smiling, and asking her
If she wanted to share my soap

BAKING MEMORY #101

(1)
The bakery was close to nowhere
In the middle of a refinery town
We made products for gas stations
I worked on a team that developed
The 39-cent super velvet loaf

(2)
Throughout the night, and early morning hours
Many topics were discussed
One of the favorites was the Holy Bible
Almost everyone in those days
Had a working knowledge of the Scriptures
Unlike the crews of today
Who are biblically illiterate

(3)

Don the florist was an odd duck

An animated character

From a television show

That never got produced

It seemed obvious to everyone except him

That he was queer

The way he looked at us young men

Our muscles and sweat, oh my

How many times did he invite me

Or one of the other lads

To swing by on a day off for brunch

And a stroll through his gardens

(4)
Amongst the crew, the most visited topic
Was Genesis Chapter Six
When the fallen angels come down to Earth
And impregnate local women
It was agreed, these unusual sex acts
Produced an offspring
That resulted in freakish mutants

(5)
Almost everyone (other than the oven crew)
Believed this unholy union
Led to the inception of giants
This is why archeologists have found
Throughout the landscape of Petra
Furniture and buildings that support
The view that freakishly large people existed
In centuries past

(6)
Don the florist seemed beyond certain
That Goliath came from the bloodline
Of fallen angels
Oh, how he would get worked up
Tugging on his ascot as he explained
(And I'm paraphrasing here)

(7)

It wasn't the five smooth stones
That toppled the giant
Nor was it the shepherd boy's accuracy
Goliath was stupid
He prayed to Dagon
A fish worshipped by Philistines
How can a God save you
If it has no arms
Limbs are generally a minimal requirement
And to think my Sunday school teacher
Viewed David as the underdog
I liked his odds from the very beginning

(8)
Unfortunately . . .
Crews like this no longer exist
Now, most of the time, conversation is muted
By isolated bakers
Who spend their mornings attached
To whatever is streaming through their earbuds

BAKING MEMORY #102

In the kitchen at the University of Moscow
I was under the tutelage of Alyona
She didn't look like a kitchen worker
She looked like a librarian
Maybe a professor, not that it matters
What did matter, or was helpful
She had partial control of the English language
At mealtime the crew scurried
But when things slowed down
Alyona encouraged me to put on my chef coat
And stroll past the students and faculty
Proof her kitchen enjoyed American influence
This stroll brought me to a table of women
Romanian, Hungarian, Bulgarian or such
Our moment surpassed a moment
Annoyance was apparent, Alyona called for my return
Face to face, she said . . .
They are bad women, they won't give you a situation
I smiled, I asked . . .
Are the Russians volunteering to give me a situation
Alyona blushed while explaining . . .
Such a question, a woman doesn't answer with words

BAKING MEMORY #103

During the rush, they ran out of buns
I brought some over, to get them through
She made the cook hook me up
With a bacon burger and Diet Coke
I mentioned to her, the last time I swung by
She wasn't here
She said she was on vacation
I asked . . . Where did you go
She said . . . The Walker
The art museum I asked
She nodded yes, for three days
Why I asked,
She said Yoko Ono had an installation
A red rotary phone, hung on the wall
It was reported, Yoko may or may not call
I asked . . . Did you talk to her
She said . . . No, I said . . . What a waste
She said . . . Not really, because . . .
A vacation with the potential of talking to Yoko
Is better than Disneyland
I didn't disagree

BAKING MEMORY #104

(1)
8 a.m. St. Patrick's Day 198?
Wife #1 sat in a dutiful position
On the stoop, I was past tired
I just got home from work
All the Irish soda bread
All the Irish soda bread
Next to her sat a puppy wagging its tail
She said . . . I know you don't like to be alone
I said . . . I'm not, I'm with you
She said . . . Not anymore, I'm moving out
Please accept this parting gesture

(2)
Nobody likes when a partner upsets the apple cart
I stood dismayed, for years I held a grudge
For years I had a chip, until it occurred to me
She had the more difficult job, carrying out a task
That opened our lives to future happiness
I try to remember her strength, each time, every time
Opinions oppose mine, with the understanding
Sometimes . . . It's in everyone's best interest
To root for the villain

BAKING MEMORY #105

(1)
While touring a book of poems
Written in support of Mexican bakers
The editor of the "TASTE" section
Told me, she could get me
A feature in the Washington Post
If I wanted
I wanted

(2)
The interview was over the phone
The guy asked this, he asked that
I did my best to come across as
Witty and relevant, while staying on point

(3)
I wasn't told, when the story would run
I wondered, I touched down at Reagan
I stayed in a budget hotel
The Architect
Other than a couple speaking Russian
In the entry-level TV room
I may have been the only guest

(4)

I arrived late

My neighborhood didn't have a liquor store

I had to address the nation's capital

Sober and alone, tucked away in a room

That offered a view of a brick wall

Across the street

Headlights found their way to this wall

Bouncing and splashing

Mixed in something between

Rain and snow, the optics were beautiful

Beautiful and surreal

(5)

I crawled into bed, I brought a book

"THE RUM DIARY"

By Hunter S. Thompson

It was his debut novel, I wondered . . .

Would some writer, someday

Travel to a city of purpose, to achieve something

Others would eventually forget

If so, I hoped they would read me

During their important moment

Because purpose holds hands with loneliness

(6)
After touring Ford's Theatre, I was numb
They had life-sized cut-outs of the assassins
Attached to the walls, I stood agog
Most of the killers were young
I learned about the assassination in first grade
It was mentioned how a group of men, did the deed
When you are in first grade, it's natural to assume
Killers are older, matured scallywags
Not young men with peach-fuzz faces
And shoulders under development
But thusly, this was that

(7)

Across the street from Ford's Theatre

Is a building with a name and purpose, I forget

But in its bowels rests the bed Lincoln laid in

After being shot, the bed his wife would see him in

Before their final goodbye

I considered the phrase 'death bed'

As I drifted into a deeper numb

"BANG" my phone went off

It was my publisher

She sounded numb as well

Momentarily, I was confused

But, eventually the publisher explained . . .

It's out, your Washington Post feature

He wrote it well, your life will never be the same

Good luck on tonight's show, and . . .

Sell a shit ton of books

(8)

The show went well

Afterwards my literary escort and I inadvertently got drunk

At a safe house

With some culprits

Who employed manners

And a flair for grace

As I took a taxi back to the Architect

I considered the night

The accomplishment

My debt to my team that made all this possible

Then I became sad

I was alone

I considered my life's journey and its current arc

How did I get here

I took notes

I smiled

This is what I came up with . . .

(9)

Sunday morning after Mass, Grandma swears, Grandpa
    laughs
Relatives will be here soon, we'll sit down for lunch at noon
When we come together, we're complete
Carry groceries from the car, Little Debbie Nutty Bars
Fresca, Tang, Quisp and Quake
Swanson Dinners, Shake & Bake
All packed neatly in Red Owl Bags
Broken dishes, stain on shirt, arguments before dessert
Cup of Sanka, Sara Lee, cribbage and Monopoly
Grandpa stops to watch the evening news
And we don't want the night to end
We don't want to be apart
The stars come out to form a canopy
Everyone is comfortable, when they're not alone
Sunday evening, kitchen's closed
Say goodbye, it's time to go
Weddings, funerals, holiday
Is the next time when we'll play
Grandma smiles waving from the street
When we come together, we're complete

BAKING MEMORY #106

(1)
Thanksgiving Eve
The crew finished up a three-day jag
Of baking 5000 pies
The only thing more tedious
Than baking 5000 pies
Is packaging 5000 pies
All those boxes, stickers
Papers and bows
With a fuzzy mug and barking dawgs
I hopped in my car and headed home

(2)
On the drive back to the Capital City
I listened to Christmas music
Then, something in my skull
Chimed into my commute
Urging me to stop at the grocery
For last-minute needs

(3)
I didn't really have to have
Anything in particular
But something in my skull urged me on
Because I was tired, Because I was lazy
Because I have money to burn
I stopped at Kowalski's
Knowing they would allow me the pleasure
Of paying 40% more than their competitors

(4)

I walked through aisles

Waiting for providence to guide me

Why was I here, what do I need

I didn't know, so I bought

Chicken wings, salad, a nutcracker dishtowel

And fluffy wife socks

What, What, What was I doing here

(5)
After an order
Equivalent to a car payment, was rung up
Something in my skull reminded me
You're running low on Jack Daniels
Lucky for me, Kowalski's has an adjoining
High-end liquor store

(6)

At a brisk clip, I entered, grabbed my bottle
Heading to a counter, where two cashiers
Rang orders with speed and precision
Both guys wore masks
Both guys had Mel Gibson – Braveheart hairdos
I set my bottle down and displayed kindness
Issuing small talk that offered little value
Other than serving as an indicator
That I wasn't a complete self-absorbed creep

(7)
During a split moment of silence
Left cashier looked at me
Greeting me with my Christian name
A salutation like this seldom happens
Most greet me by my moniker
I knew, I knew this guy
But with that mask on, it was hard to tell

(8)
After chatting this and that, it came to me
Left cashier was Boy Zoro
A man I met 25 years previous
A man who studied baking in Italy
There was little not to love about Boy Zoro
He was the smartest person
In most of the rooms he occupied

(9)
After a couple years, Boy Zoro
Gave up my dream
Of playing Watson to my Holmes
I hadn't seen him in ages
I had so many questions
But I was fearful because
Anything I asked him about him
Could be perceived as
Disappointed dad dialogue
So . . . as he slid my bottle into a sleeve
I reminded him how much I liked his mother
A comment which caused him to drop his mask
And flash me a smile that indicated
He was happy and doing his best

(10)

I have much to be thankful for

BAKING MEMORY #107

(1)
As one can imagine, there's much to tell
Government recruitment
Government scopes
Service to Uncle Sam
Suiting up in bakers' whites
Amidst the Asiatic Arctic
Amidst the Diamond City
Bodyguards
Vodka
Pig dung cigarettes
Murder trials
White nights
Dog packs
The monthly shower
Suicides and World Cup Soccer
As one can imagine, there's much to tell
But let's not bypass the puberty of adventure
Let's remember, every journey of merit
Starts off at an Airport Bar
3-2-1 . . .

(2)

Her nametag announced her as Viv
As did her raspy voice
She placed a coaster in front of me
And stared while asking
Brave sailor, where will your journey take you
When I mentioned I was off to Siberia
She adjusted her apron and said
Nobody goes there, I would know
But if the Ivans let you return, Tuesdays are my day off
A night with Viv was illusion
Something to which my wife would object
But, the prospect was alluring, because like me,
Viv was a lout, but, if fantasy became reality
We'd come home from dinner parties
Parade ourselves upstairs
And while she began to take off her jewelry
She'd start a fight, I just couldn't win
And maybe that's the reason these moments
Remain nothing more than possibilities
Enough to occupy the moment
Until another sailor comes along

BAKING MEMORY #108

Scarto delivered bread
Making morning drops when accounts opened
Clients called frequently
Commenting how handsome Scarto was
Others said . . . Scarto was a dick
But it didn't much matter
Because he was so handsome
Scarto delivered bread
Eventually his son signed on too
Like free-spirited bards
They navigated the metro daily
Breaking bread and breaking hearts
One day, that day, when fortune turned
Scarto got jumped by an assailant
Who smashed Scarto's face with a brick
Breaking his cheekbone, crushing his beauty
A face caved in
After surgery, we asked Scarto
To resume his route, he declined saying . . .
I won't let people see me like this

BAKING MEMORY #109

(1)
When he wasn't on the Rez
Or at vocational school
Joe the Mohican picked up shifts
Pounding out dough with me and the Mexicans
This went on, on and off
Over the course of several years
Joe the Mohican was quiet by nature
Seldom offering opinions or advice
All the more reason, I stood in shock
When he flipped off Oso, the bench foreman
While announcing . . . Fuck You
At a decibel I hadn't heard him utilize
Weeks went by, months did too
Until the day the television news
Announced our long-tenured bakery
Failed an ICE audit
We were granted ten days of tolerance
Before we had to disband

(2)

The following day, hearts were heavy
Hearts were broken, I was on the ovens when I noticed
Joe the Mohican had returned
To my surprise, he was hugging Oso
To my surprise, he tied on an apron
I was confused, happy, but confused
Joe the Mohican smiled, assuring me . . .
There is no way I'm going to let you guys sink
Without me
Joe the Mohican transcends rules and logic
I am proud to call him friend
Mohicans in St. Paul are rare
But friends who volunteer
To go down with the ship are priceless
I love Joe the Mohican
And I want you to love him too

BAKING MEMORY #110

(1)
On the same evening of the Academy Awards
The stars in Minneapolis fall from the sky
And make their way to Hennepin Avenue
Toward the Pantages Theatre
Where the best of the best put on
A hospitality awards show where . . .
Achievements are awarded
And food service workers are honored
Over 1000 will attend
Dressing rooms, sound checks
Gossip and bullshit, and as you might imagine
The best backstage spread you can imagine
After my book of poems against ICE
Won the Midwest Book Award
Somebody had the idea
To let me open and close the show

(2)

Reading for poets is a cinch
But truth be told, I was terrified
To share my heart, with my industry
Damn those lights were bright
I couldn't see a thing
But it was weird, I could hear 1000 people
People made noises, I couldn't see a thing
But somehow I managed
To hear the voice of Joe the Mohican
Asking a random question
For whatever reason, that grounded me enough
To get comfortable enough, to do me
To lift my fist in the air, state my name
And let the crowd know . . .
I stand with Mexicans
The response was overwhelming
If I left that stage with tears in my eyes
I would never admit it
So don't bother asking *wink*

BAKING MEMORY #111

(1)
FACT: On June 3rd, 1990
Soviet President Mikhail Gorbachev
Touched down in the Twin Cities
In a red, white and blue Aeroflot jet
For the first time in a long time
Minnesota was back
In the international spotlight
Everybody was curious why Gorbachev
Agreed to a six-hour layover here
Before joining President Reagan in California

(2)
As usual, answers were not given
Nor did it matter, as Gorbymania
Was out of control
And sweeping across America
Everybody – Everybody
Everybody wanted a piece of Gorbachev's layover

(3)
Hundreds of VIPs ranging from Fritz Mondale
To pre-approved CEOs, waited to pimp their wares
While standing in uncharacteristic weather
That resembled a Siberian cold front
The temperature was 49 degrees
The skies were gray and drizzling
As the beautiful mob stood huddling close
For warmth and a view

(4)
On the tarmac, next to a bunch of Marines
All of them packing major heat
All of us sensed this had to be the event of the season
Even Cher offered to fly in from Chicago
But her request was denied

(5)
A local farmer remembered that Gorbachev
Was once a Soviet agriculture secretary
And offered to bring an 850# boar
To any spot along the motorcade
To be admired
That idea was also shot down

(6)
I even heard a woman who became a bride that day
Offered to save Gorby a dance
But the diplomat guest didn't have enough time
To partake of the hospitality offered

(7)

I, in an offhanded way, was the exception

(8)

I first found out about Gorbachev's visit
When I was working at a bakery on West 7th
Bloodline to the Capital City
The Governor's mansion was one of our accounts
I was told that Governor Rudy Perpich
(A Croatian-American)
Wanted to have a special loaf designed
For a ceremony, where he and Gorby
Would break bread
Together, as a symbol of peace

(9)

That's where I came in

(10)
The symbol of peace, the special bread
Couldn't come off the grocery store shelf
That would be savage
These world leaders were in the milling capital
Of the free world
This event demanded a loaf, a perfect loaf
That would transcend all expectations

(11)

When you design culinary dishes

For visiting dignitaries

You have two options

You can try to replicate

Something from their homeland

Or you can create something indigenous to yours

I opted for the latter

(12)
After hearing Gorby was excited
To visit Reagan's ranch
It was reported Gorby was enthralled
With Native Americans
And wanted to find out more about their history
From America's favorite cowboy actor

(13)

Like a symphony conductor, I orchestrated

Searching the finest ingredients

Our state had to offer

Projects like this are a blast because . . .

You have no budget

Everybody wants you to get

The best ingredients money can buy

(14)
During the week leading to the arrival
We had visits from intimidating thugs
Who may have been
FBI or KGB
These people don't hand out business cards
I was a young man, I took no offense
While these inspectors grilled me with questions
While sifting through our ingredient bins

(15)
I was not there, at the event
I was after all, just the baker
But imagine in your mind's eye
The President of Russia
Biting into a slice of my bread
With just a dab of that good Minnesota butter on it
Eyes closed, as he nods in the affirmative
Sealing friendship between the two leaders

(16)
Had I not done my job properly
Who's to say
There might have been Soviet missiles
Pointed towards our country
Pointed towards your home
This very moment

BAKING MEMORY #112

(1)

On the west bank, we were flooded
With the presence of Somali people
Punk rock pilgrims
And clouds that cast shadows
Doubling as Bob Dylan's ghost
Spano carried a backpack containing
Cans of beer, chess boards and pieces
A two-player game clock
Cigarettes and a roll of SweeTarts
After stepping into the Wienery Restaurant
I declared . . . Food Workers Chess Club begins
In 3-2-1

(2)

The proprietor ushered us in, sat us at a counter

Overhead, I spied plastic bins containing jail bracelets

That recently incarcerated people traded

For a free breakfast and warm conversation

The proprietor was a family man

His wife was in law school

Their two sons stopped by frequently

Laying siege on clientele, with modified lightsabers

One of the boys was named Jesus Tarzan

The other brother's name was less imaginative

The lads inspired their father to drop his spatula

And waltz over to the piano to play standards

Which were above his customers' pay grade

(3)

Food Workers Chess Club wasn't advertis

It was a word-of-mouth thing

It happened when it happened

Our game was blitz

Two minutes per side, buck a shot

But once word got out, Ameripride linen drivers

And liquor store cashiers

Asked if they could join in

4)
I won a bunch, I lost a bunch
But the highlight of my chess career
Was my single win over Spano
In food service terms
It was like beating Bobby Fischer
Spano could have told you, he was distracted
We were at Donovan's Pub, getting drunk
In preparation for a New York Dolls show
He spotted me two pawns
A guy stood by our booth
Singing U2 songs and kissing people
On top of their skulls
Spano ended up scrapping with the lout
In the confusion, he hung his queen
Realizing his predicament, he resigned
Spano could have reminded me
He had beat me 1000 consecutive times
Instead, he handed me a dollar
And told me I played a good game

BAKING MEMORY #113

I drove an old car to a new job
Parked behind the bakery, boots crunched ice
Breath was vapor, I was cold
Next to the delivery truck, lying in a snow bank
Was an old woman
Not wanting to be an upstart, or intrude
I approached and inquired about her status
Permission was granted to hoist, upon doing this
I noticed this 80ish-year-old woman
Was wearing leather pants and a beehive wig
She introduced herself as Myrtle
A self-proclaimed spinster
Who lived in DC with her sister
Both were high-end secretaries
During the FDR administration
Several hours after my shift started
Myrtle walked into the bakery
With a plate of cookies, asking for Danny
After claiming my gift and Myrtle returned home
The bread jackals stared and grinned
While I stared down at the floor knowing
I had entered Jerusalem on the back of an ass

BAKING MEMORY #114

In the Grand Hotel, decorum is mandated
On smudged placards, hung over the apron hamper
Unfortunately for those involved
The rules weren't clear to me
I was the caterer's last-minute hire
I entered the event center
As guests filled in, my task was to place
Cheesecake centerpieces on tables
Cookies and Cream here, Raspberry Swirl there
When it was time to distribute the Key Lime version
I approached a table for twelve, its only occupants
Were a small boy and an old woman
The boy was drawing pictures
Pictures of tanks, I asked if they were Panzers
The old lady admonished me with a reminder
It was poor form for staff to engage those they served
Insulted and angry, I urged the boy to draw an airplane
And have it drop a bomb on his granny
The boy laughed, I was escorted out
Forfeiting a day's wages

BAKING MEMORY #115

(1)
Poets are poets, because they are cowards
Not in each aspect of their demeanor
Just ones that wound them enough
To become poets
Case in point . . . me
The village baker
The man who would have been king
Had he found the handle on intimacy
Building monuments is easy
Legacies, a breeze
But knowing how to connect to souls
Yikes, not so much
Trying for connection
Hoping for understanding
I haven't cracked the code, so . . .
I simply go to locations
Filled with people I trust
If they aren't present
I might read a book in their parking lot

(2)

There's a German Inn on the Southside
Run by a family and select ruffians
Five years ago, six years ago, or was it seven
The Inn prepared to celebrate its 50th birthday
I grabbed eye goggles, Silpat pads, caustic soda
I had been given the privilege
Of making pretzel bread
The Hustle – The Bustle, it's hard to explain
Generosity, yelling, jokes and confusion
Doused with purpose, battered with joy
When my task was complete
I was told by a daughter
If I returned the following day
I could make sausage links
With the father

(3)

The following morning, I suited up
Crossed the river, entered the cooler
Just before sunrise. Pops joined me
For the first half hour, we didn't talk sausage
He gathered ingredients and told me
He'd be going out of business soon
Because he refused to put TVs
In the dining room or bar
And according to those who keep stride
With modern living
Nothing is valued more than television
He told me what it was like
To be a German living in America
During the 50s
He told me about his boat
As well as the failed Twins pitching staff
Then he fell silent and considered
In the silence, I remember thinking
How happy I would be today
If this man had been my father

(4)
I learned 90% of ingredients in sausage are basic
It's the 10% that will define their distinction
I learned the value of muscle memory
As I watched a man three times the age of his staff
Twist bratwurst casings
Three times faster than his agile crew
I learned, even though I didn't have the words
To express my gratitude for inclusion
It no longer mattered
I could feel the glow
That takes place in a kitchen filled with hope
Over my career, I've baked for Presidents
And dignitaries, that was fine
But baking with the Germans meant more
Maybe because I finally realized
In life . . . If you don't get what you want
Knowing what you want has merit

BAKING MEMORY #116

Midnight, sunshine, springtime, Siberia
In a field, I sit with my bodyguard
A carton of Marlboros, our interpreter
A bottle of whiskey and a bag of brioche
Grass and bramble, bent and gnarled
Grass and bramble, brown and gray
The view is desolate and lonely
I am waiting for a pack of wild dogs
Which I will feed bread
The bodyguard warns me
If the locals find out I'm giving food
To these beasts, a price will be paid
I mumble to the interpreter, she reports to our guard
If you want Jack Daniels, you must comply
The bodyguard nods in agreement and explains
He has saved for years to buy this land
After being released from prison, then he asks . . .
Does America have a place as beautiful
I sat and thought, sat and smoked
Until it occurred to me
Iowa

BAKING MEMORY #117

Before my last day of baking
I was told to go to Gorky Park
On a bench I waited for my interpreter
She was late, old men fished a pond
Using corn for bait
On a bench, I waited and smoked a Marlboro
A pretty woman sat next to me
And helped herself to my cigarettes
There were other benches, empty benches
But she chose mine, we smoked in silence
She looked away, looked up, exhaling
And for reasons I can't explain, I deduced
She would never have to claim another's hardships
She looked away, she looked up, transfixed
A kaleidoscope of butterflies appeared from nowhere
Their movement didn't denote grace or unison
They appeared to battle
My interpreter arrived, examined my companion
I expressed I'd like to send her a message
The interpreter groaned and implied, it's pointless
She knows everything you are thinking
We must go

BAKING MEMORY #118

(1)
I don't know how they pull it off, but . . .
The Kaanapali Hotel Maui is . . .
So pink, so modern, so retro
Contains a swag that's hard to describe
On the beachfront, a stellar restaurant
Fish, eggs, pineapples and mango
On the beachfront, couples relax
Enjoying paradise, enjoying sunrise
I, on the other hand, wait in the atrium
Amidst small kiosks
Filled with wares made in-house
I would like to be on the beachfront
But, I am partnered with a wife
Who embraces morning with glacial speed
A habit that forces me to meander
I wait, I drink espresso rocking back and forth
Staring at an open window on the kitchen line
Where a guy 50 shows a guy 20
How to scoop muffins properly

(2)
Day after day, the routine continues
Toward the end of the week, 50 Guy
Barks out an invitation for me to join him
I accepted
Going into another baker's domain
Isn't much different
Than peeking behind a magician's table
Miracles and mysteries, mystery and intrigue
50 Guy showed me this, told me that
I learned so much, we had a few laughs
At a point where it seemed natural
To go our separate ways
20 Guy asked 50 Guy
What made you invite someone
You never met, into our kitchen
50 Guy answered . . . He watched us all week
I knew he had to be food service
And being food service, you can bet
He'll never have enough money to visit again
Then 50 Guy smiled
And thanked me for my appreciation

BAKING MEMORY #119

Whatever action proceeds pandemonium
Is exactly what occurred
Outside by the donut dumpster
In front of me, a German and an African
Stood despondent, staring at the squirrel
Who died, clinging to the dumpster
Trying to pull itself out
It should have escaped easily
I've never seen anything dead, look so alive
Above perched a crow, as big as a terrier
Cawing with unprecedented volume
The German wondered, would the crow swoop down
And vulture the rodent corpse
None of us liked that idea much
And considered placing the squirrel
Inside the dumpster and closing the lid
Until the African mused thoughtfully . . .
Perhaps it would be best, to let it be
Its brothers and sisters are probably looking for him
They deserve to know
We returned to the bakery
Finishing our shifts with empty hearts

BAKING MEMORY #120

Jamal McDuff was handsome and athletic
He proclaimed himself to be
St. Paul's Blackest Irishman
I gathered, like some of us
He was struggling to make ends meet
Yet, his shallow pockets never prevented him
From offering me a sandwich
Or a Diet Pepsi
Jamal McDuff closed the ovens
On the shifts I didn't
We rotated every night
The task was arduous
Yet he approached his fate
With more dignity than I
Jamal McDuff was a Black man
Driving home at 2 a.m. in a black Toyota
I was a white guy, in a white Toyota
Who left at the same time
During the summer of '86
The cops pulled Jamal over six times
As he tried to make his way home
I was never stopped

BAKING MEMORY #121

(1)
If you've been in the show
If you've worked hospitality, odds are
You were subjected to the abuse
And had to slide on a "freezer coat"
Rationalizing the humility
By reassuring yourself
It was the lesser of two evils

(2)
Who's to say why a bakery in St. Paul
Would have a freezer coat
Covered with San Francisco 49ers emblems
Nobody remembered who brought it
How the hood got torn
Or if the traces of black goo
Were mold or frozen mechanics' grease
One of the bread jackals assured us all
If that freezer coat was carbon tested
It was certain to date back
To the Napoleonic Wars
I didn't disagree

(3)

A woman with five cats

The guy allergic to antiperspirant

A pink guy who looked like Gary Busey

A guy who hung himself

Some guy who got AIDS

Some guy who followed Jesus

A woman who ate fish heads

A man who molded bread animals

The freezer coat wasn't an initiation

It was a necessity

(4)

The worst time to get freezer detail
Was July or August
After some sweaty goon occupied its presence
Leaving behind a film cold and slimy
Pauly Detroit once pointed out
Static flour on the sleeve
That froze, thawed, and froze
Until it thawed once more
Created tiny bugs, it's not hard to realize
Why I'm not particularly fond of the 49ers

BAKING MEMORY #122

Sandra "The Bandit" spoke seldom at most
But when she did, her statements held weight
Statements such as . . .
Smelling Christmas trees in Minnesota
Is better than smelling Christmas trees in New Mexico
Christmas trees mixed with cold air
Create a moment you'll never capture when it's hot
Speaking of capture
Sandra "The Bandit" was captured
Committing a heist with her boyfriend
Who was a security guard at a building
Which he and Sandra "The Bandit" tried to rob
However, the caper was foiled
By another security guard
Who I'm willing to bet
Didn't have a girlfriend as interesting
As Sandra "The Bandit"

BAKING MEMORY #123

(1)
Bubba was a Swede
Blonde hair, thick mustache
If his hair had been brown
He would have been the spitting image
Of a pint-sized Marlboro Man
Bubba taught me many things
How to run ovens
How to get promoted
How to avoid the loneliness
Of being a third-shift oven man
He told me the best way
To make the time pass quickly
Was to have conversations
In your head with dead people
The suggestion was more than brilliant
It was second nature
Throughout my youth, much of my time
Was engaged in conversations
With Jesus and Houdini

(2)

In second grade, through a cracked door
I overheard the counselor tell mother
We don't think he's retarded . . . but
As she closed the office door completely
It left me to wonder if this announcement
Should cause shame or relief
Next they ran a battery of tests concluding with the question
What type of man do you admire
I responded . . . Jesus and Houdini
The kid-shrink smiled as she turned to my mother
With the following prognosis . . .
It's fortunate you have a child of faith
Churches have great social service programs
At that, my mother terminated the interview
As we climbed into the car, and I fastened my seatbelt
I could see she was frustrated
When I asked if I did something wrong
She nearly cried and hugged me really tight
While telling me . . .
I'll find the money somewhere
To get you those magic lessons
I'd rather take my chances with the magician

BAKING MEMORY #124

(1)
I brought samples to Zander's Café
Its namesake disregarded my gifts
And motioned me to follow him
Into a basement that doubled
As a wine cellar
I mentioned I'd never seen so many bottles
He said . . .
Last month I got rid of half this amount
I had to come to terms with the fact
Minnesota isn't New York
They don't take wine seriously
Midwesterners don't enjoy reading
Their entire catalog of options
My wine menu had 16 pages, but . . .
90% of the pours ordered
Were ordered off the front page

(2)

I brought bread samples to Zander's Café
Its namesake disregarded my gifts
And turned me on to a mosaic soup
I want to say three flavors
Puree, colored green, white and orange
What were those flavors
Sweet Pea, Potato, Butternut Squash
Sweet Pea, Potato, Carrot
Watercress, Potato, Carrot
Gosh, now that I think of it
Maybe there was a beet component
Moral of the story
It's not essential to remember ingredients
When remembering your favorite meals
But it is considered good form
To remember who made it

(3)
At Zander's Café
The namesake celebrated his best friend
A Chihuahua, by fashioning Chihuahua cookies
He gave to guests at the completion of their meals
Truthfully, it didn't have to be an entrée
Even if you ordered appetizers
Salad, drinks or dessert
With your bill came the Chihuahua cookie
This ritual produced smiles
Until the unthinkable occurred
The pint-sized pup was struck down and killed
By a hit-and-run driver
At first we worried about the namesake
But after healing mended hearts
We considered if the cookies would continue
Everybody in the industry waited, and wondered
To my delight, the next time I stopped by
After this and that, my bill came
As did my Chihuahua cookie
Attached to a set of flapping angel wings

BAKING MEMORY #125

Friday, the ringmaster passed out checks

Warning us to stay out of trouble, once bread crew finished

The circus started, usually at the dough mixer's house

Guns N' Roses, Faith No More, whiskey and weed

Nobody pulled out the nose candy

Until the closing oven man was able to join

Under the big top, we blew off steam

But once the ritual became routine

Snorting was replaced with needles

An automatic cue for my departure

One evening, when I saw a clown

Scoring smack in the driveway

I was gone, only to find out Sunday

A makeshift orgy started after I left

Accusations were made over who touched who

Whether there was consent or not

Instead of bringing in the cops

The alleged victim brought their plea

To the ringmaster who promised to investigate

However, before justice was served

The ringmaster fell off some bad horse, never to rise again

BAKING MEMORY #126

In a world without internet, the following occurred
At the production bench, Douglas mentioned . . .
A woman at the bus stop said I looked adorable
Standing akimbo, Douglas confessed . . .
I don't know what akimbo means
Bernie Banks said . . .
It's code, for dude-on-dude activities
Marci White said . . .
It sounds ninja
Tre Phillips said . . .
Nobody expects you to be smart
You're a baker, not an English teacher
The comments made Douglas fume
In a huff, he asked . . .
Do you guys know the definition of "akimbo"
Or are you too stupid too
Most of us burst out laughing
But to Douglas' satisfaction
Our crew was indicted
By our inability to produce an answer

BAKING MEMORY #127

Two geese, they're both honking
Bringing joy, at least to me
They're back, searching for food
The dumpster is empty
I toss them milk buns
The oven man indicates my gesture
Is an open invitation to trouble
The pleasure was mine
How natural they seem
Relaxed in their stance
Waiting for nothing to happen
Our shift is over
One by one, bakers drive away
Until I am left alone, in my car
Staring at two geese
Taking mental note of a nobility
Silence, time passes, nobody moves
I set my gaze, and let it sink in
Knowing eventually, I will forget them
Like everything else

BAKING MEMORY #128

Hector the Cuban can only blame himself
He ate alone, smoked alone
And never had cocktails with the crew
On a Friday night, a busy night, frosty night
Temperatures skirting around sub-zero
Two cops entered our production space
With a warrant for Hector the Cuban
Who didn't put up a fight, he simply asked . . .
If he could grab his coat from the bathroom
The cops said yes, Hector slammed the door
Locked it, the cops bolted, the crew fell silent
Enough to hear what sounded like rats in the rafters
From the middle of the bakery came "KABOOM"
The ceiling burst, Hector fell from the sky
Until a stack of bread broke his fall
In a single motion, he bounced to his feet
Running, hiding in the walk-in cooler
Begging us to keep his secret
When the cops returned, each and every baker
Displayed an outstretched finger, pointed toward the cooler
Hector the Cuban can only blame himself

BAKING MEMORY #129

(1)
At the Mill City Museum
I lectured about dog biscuits
A couple introduced themselves
The wife explained
Recently they toured Italy
In an unnamed town, they met a woman
An older woman who was poor and proud
She refused charity
Instead she secured leashes and collars
And rented them to tourists
Who could momentarily adopt
One of many stray dogs
While letting the older woman
Maintain her dignity
Gosh, what a story
Gosh, what a concept
Leash and collar

(2)

From the Siberian arctic to the Black Sea
Packs of dogs run wild
All sizes, all breeds, they walk aimlessly
Doing dog things, thinking dog thoughts
At the beach in Gelendzhik
I witnessed five or six dogs
Growling, fighting over a fish, washed up on shore
A small dog stood at the back of the pack
Without a chance to compete
A Corgi offshoot, striking a shabby form
That wouldn't be found endearing
By Disney or the Queen
I had been to Russia before
I understood their disdain towards dogs
They viewed them like
A New Yorker views rats
I had been to Russia before
I came equipped, out of my backpack
I produced a collar and leash

(3)

I named the Corgi, Mouse
Every day before and after
My baking shift
At a converted tank factory
I'd leash up the mutt
And parade across the boardwalk
Our presence was magnetic
Women swooned, children gushed
Women whispered, children giggled
As I fed Mouse delicacies
Purchased at higher-end kiosks

(4)

It didn't take long for that ritual to become routine
Residents camped out
To receive glad tidings from America
While offering treats and belly rubs to Mouse
When my work contract expired
A young street urchin named Victor asked . . .
What would become of Mouse
Would I take him back to America
I explained, governments would forbid this
After all, Mouse was a Russian
And loved the sea
Then, after tousling the urchin's hair
I reminded him, Mouse was a free dog
As I bent down to remove the collar
Victor the sweet urchin began to cry
Informing me . . .
If you take off his collar
He'll think you don't love him anymore
My interpreter hugged the kid
As I handed him the leash

BAKING MEMORY #130

Mother, daughter, lean on the counter
KA-CHING . . . cashier rings up
20 dozen donuts and a cheesecake
I loaded their van
I asked . . . why so many donuts
Mother says . . . Daughter's getting married tomorrow
Daughter says . . . Who knew
My wedding would be filled
With pandemic and snow
Both faces were deadpan, until . . .
I announced . . . A hundred years ago
I got married, and . . .
I don't remember the weather
Or who attended, the only thing I do remember
Is my bride, she was beautiful
Almost as beautiful as today
Mother smiled and said . . . Thanks
Daughter rolled her eyes
But smiled, before pulling away
Into an abundance of flakes
Wetter than snow

BAKING MEMORY #131

At the peak of my career
In an era when I controlled my destiny
I made a decision, I wanted to do more
Than make money and gather acclaim
I talked to a woman, who told me about a guy
Who worked for an organization
That employed young men
Who were formerly incarcerated
I bought into the program, with the idea
I would help these guys salvage, or better yet
Resurrect their lives over the course of several years
I worked with a couple dozen of these men
None of them were able to stay clean
Every one of them returned to prison
The result was soul crushing
I confessed to my wife, I had failed
She reminded me, everything has perspective
And in fairness to the situation
I needed to remember
None of us has the power to grant healing
But we can offer moments worth remembering

BAKING MEMORY #132

Pete the butcher was a baker, built small
But he possessed a "freak out factor"
That kept the bread jackals at bay
He might have been a Turk, or possibly from Senegal
He was older, a product of the 60s
Peace, Love & Hare Krishna
He seldom spoke, but when he did
It sounded sacred, like something off a scroll
When I torched my knee in a fight
I limped like an invalid, it hurt so much
I made an appointment for a MRI
Even though I was broke and uninsured
Pete the butcher told me to forego
Western medicine and join him at his house
His wife would heal me, placing needles in my body
I became a pin cushion, the following day, it hurt so much
The day after that, I was back to normal
Not long after, I returned to Pete the butcher's house
I tried to pay his wife with cash, she explained . . .
If I accept money, it won't heal properly

BAKING MEMORY #133

Christmas, bakery closed
Family suggested the movies
They chose "LES MISERABLES"
To my surprise, the theater was packed
In the concession line, next to me
Two guys, big guys, same size as me
One of the two said to the other . . .
Russell Crowe's turned into an operatic fop
I ignored the comment, until I couldn't
I mentioned . . . Don't talk shit about Russell Crowe
He's the God-D Gladiator, who are you
The two guys stared, until one guy said . . .
I don't recall asking your opinion
I stepped forward, ill-equipped popcorn makers
Pleaded for calm, in the climax of hostility
My son said . . . Father, you're not in a bakery
You're in the world, and it's Christmas
The room fell quiet, people stared at me
The repentant goon, who eventually realized
He wasn't in a bakery, he was in the world
And it was Christmas

BAKING MEMORY #134

If you called Mik a chef, he'd bust you in the chops
He was a cook, earning a living at a Chicago Bears sports bar
Marco was a writer, business and tech
He loved to gush over how Viggo Mortensen
Wrote a forward for his book of poems
We assembled at the Tavern on Grand
Three amigos, each surpassing six feet
After "Peaches" our balding barkeep
Served us our second cocktail, two men burst through
    the door
Charging our friend Peaches, shaking fists and screaming
    threats
Mik bounced out of the booth, I followed
Within moments, the assailants were tossed
Fleeing down the sidewalk, tails between their legs
As I turned around, I saw Marco sitting
He never joined the ranks who protected
The most important man in the room
The bartender . . . our bartender
Shaking my head, I said to Mik . . .
Shit goes down, writers gonna write, nothing more
But line cooks, they'll have your back, every time

BAKING MEMORY #135

(1)
After surgery the doctor asked if I used to box
I answered . . . a little
The doctor explained . . . A little was enough
To create a landslide of damage
Your septum has been broken in no fewer than six places
We have done our best to reconstruct and stretch
   the septum
To keep this secure, I will insert plastic rods
The size of your middle finger, one in each nasal cavity
Then we will stitch the nostrils
Partially shut, you will be able to breathe
But every two hours, for 100 hours
You will have to moisten the cavities
With prescribed solution
I thought, I froze before asking . . .
Four days with rods in my head
I'm not sure I will be able to cope
The doctor smiled and offered assurance
I've done this procedure many times
You're going to be "A-OK"
Then he handed me a prescription for morphine

(2)

When you have been awake every two hours

For 100 hours, you get goofy

Think white nights or insomnia

But it was spring, it was warm

Gentle breeze, light rain

People called, I didn't answer

When you have morphine . . .

You're sitting at God's throne, with explicit permission

To taste and touch, as much as one can

Without need of repentance, I exercised this prerogative
    by . . .

Driving in the middle of the night

Stopping at White Castle to buy sliders

For homeless and loners

Some people accepted the gifts

Others noticed the rods in my head

A sight which forced them to scram

In the morning, I'd drive breakfast sandwiches

To the bakery, to the bread jackals

Who affectionately advised me . . .

Go the fuck home

BAKING MEMORY #136

(1)
It was a big deal, I was about to be launched
In City Pages
By a James Beard Award-winning writer
On the morning the story dropped
I rushed to the coffee shop, bought espresso
And grabbed several City Pages
When I got home, nobody was home, the TV was on
The Johnny Cash "Hurt" video was in progress
I watched it, it finished, the MTV VJ announced
Johnny Cash had died, I set the City Pages down
I didn't know how to respond
Death had foiled my morning

(2)
I wanted to read about me
I wanted to look at pictures
Of me, staring back at me
But it seemed futile
Johnny Cash was dead
Several hours passed, hours of moping
I resigned to simply float
Through mourning and memories
Anchored in Johnny, Anchored in Joy
But then a new person came on TV
And ruined this moment
That already ruined my day earlier
The person announced . . .
Television personality and comedian
John Ritter has passed away
The story was breaking
Within moments, America shifted
Its attention from the Man in Black
To a washed-out sitcom star

(3)

It was too early to get drunk

So I decided not to, but I took a shot

And flipped the station back to MTV

I didn't know what to do

I did nothing, nothing with no end in sight

Tick – Tock, Tick – Tock

Just as I was about to sink into the mist

Sheryl Crow was on the tube, she said . . .

Johnny Cash was almost Biblical

I winced, the comment seemed contrived

My level of annoyance rose

Then Anthony from the Red Hot Chili Peppers

Flashed a facial expression and announced

Johnny Cash loved me, he was my friend

This statement healed me instantly

So much so, I shut off the television

Sat on the couch, and read about me

BAKING MEMORY #137

Due to government incentives, the bakery owner hired
Johnny Reebok, a man as big as a bear
But he was sweatier, and had more fur
Johnny Reebok was "touched by angels"
He was simple but strong
Originally they hired him as a driver
But he crashed a truck, he was over his head, but . . .
Due to government incentives
He was rotated to the bake staff
Where he was over his head
His inability to execute created frustration
So much so, that after a reprimand
He came after me, within a brief moment
I saw . . . the staff smirking
Johnny fuming, foaming frothy spittle chunks
From the corners of his mouth
He grabbed me, squeezed me like a vice
As my soul began to dismount
I managed to break an arm free
And punched his face, until release
The following day came a two-day suspension
For slugging a guy "touched by angels"

BAKING MEMORY #138

Shaquille took the bus in from Midway
He usually asked for overtime
He never missed a shift
On his 30th birthday, he confessed
He'd spent half his life behind bars
Each day for lunch, he consumed
Cheetos and fruit punch . . . every day!
One afternoon I passed him
As I was preparing to eat a celery stalk
Shaquille marveled at its huge leaf
He grinned, he roared
What the fuck is that, baby
I thought he was joking, until I realized he wasn't
A coworker from his neighborhood
Explained they didn't sell food-food
At the corner store
Several months later Shaquille finished a shift
On his way home he was intercepted by thugs
Thugs who were former rivals
Bang – Bang, a rival fell to the asphalt
Shaquille was sent back to a system
That never gave him a fair chance

BAKING MEMORY #139

(1)
I didn't know Lyle Bender from Adam
When he entered my office
Wearing a checkered sport coat
And a well-rehearsed smile
First it was small talk
Then he hemmed and hawed
Before he dropped a pitch
That was guaranteed
To improve my standing
With my community
As well as . . .
The Heavenly Creator

(2)
Let's get down to brass tacks
He got down to business
Handing me a business card
Containing a P.O. box
Instead of an address
Sure, more than likely
The guy was a flim-flam artist
I know that I knew better
But that checkered sport coat
And well-rehearsed smile
Were hard to resist
Submitted below, for your approval
Lyle Bender's pitch

(3)
I can tell you're a man
Who loves his country
Who loves his Lord
And I'm sure you know, it isn't a sin
To receive bounty tenfold
After giving to your father
Consider this . . .
Soldiers deployed across seas
Soldiers in battle, giving their all
Passing through hell, defending liberty
The least we could do, is give them tools
To claim victory while easing their souls
Let's expedite their success by creating an . . .
"All in one eucharist"
Instead of sending wafers and wine
Let's use the wine, instead of water
To bind the eucharist, just think of it
Body of Christ, Blood of Christ

(4)

Call me Klecko, call me rube
I did it, without a contract
I forged ahead, getting ingredients
Doing research and development on my dime
During these trials and tribulations
I came to some interesting conclusions
Type of wine, type of cracker
Percentages, oven temps
And of course . . .
The secret ingredient
Once this was gathered
I sent an invoice to Lyle's P.O. box
He called and quibbled
Over my numbers and science
Even though I gave him rock-bottom prices
He refused to reimburse me
While reminding me what happens
To those who withhold joy to the Father

(5)

I should have got over it
Let Go and Let God
I should have got over it
And not involved my children
Who I paid a dollar a picture
To grab paper and crayons
And draw images of Hell
If the pictures were super scary
Bonuses were awarded
When the collection was gathered
In childish scrawl, I placed words like . . .
Liar – Thief – Glutton and Viper
Across the headline slot
For ten consecutive days
I walked one of those artworks
To the corner mailbox
And sent them to Lyle
Who responded with a note saying . . .
I was foul and senseless
I didn't disagree

BAKING MEMORY #140

She was a reputable newspaper journalist
Who came to the bakery to discuss bread
Just the facts – Just the facts
It was easy to deduce, she was on a quest
In addition to building a brick oven
In her back yard, she was able to produce
The greatest sourdough I ever tasted
She had Nordic lineage and was Lutheran
So it took time for conversation to thaw
But once it did . . . Eureka
She discussed . . .
Episodes of "Little House on the Prairie"
The new ski jump in Oslo
Groom cakes, and Gloria Steinem's apartment
She understood the importance of listening
To the voice of dough, and its silence
Due to my Polish lineage and Catholic upbringing
My social dexterity remains unbalanced
But if, on the unlikely chance, I regain my footing
I might tell her . . . The only thing better
Than drinking vodka in Moscow
Is baking with your bestie in St. Paul

BAKING MEMORY #141

I read a book, I read a blog
Indicating, during his final years
John replaced music with bread baking
His guitar served no purpose
He hung it on the wall
The only thing that got him off
Flour, water, salt and yeast
Flour, water, salt and yeast
It's been reported
John Lennon said . . .
Making good bread
Is something even a Beatle
Can be proud of

BAKING MEMORY #142

(1)
I talked to a chef, who knew a guy
Who filled out backstage riders
For many of the Twin Cities' top venues
The "Shopper Guy" was cordial when we met
He was gracious enough to let me tag along
On an upcoming gig
I was rooting for Rod Stewart
Pink Floyd or Eminem
I got stuck with Blue Man Group
Oh well, beggars can't be choosers

(2)

I met Shopper Guy in the primary kitchen

Of the Xcel Center

I wasn't sure what Shopper Guy would look like

He looked like an eighth-grade math teacher

Shopper Guy had me hop in his Buick

While telling me we would be shopping

At a half dozen destinations

The first thing he said was . . .

The Van Halen M&M thing was a rumor

Nobody had to sort through their candy

He went on to reveal . . .

Most celebrities aren't douchebags

Then he paused before mentioning

But then there's Madonna

She's a piece of work

(3)
I sat, I smiled
Flashing my "do tell" look
Shopper Guy was anxious to please
Neil Diamond, Barbra Streisand, they're pro
They'll ask for "x-amount" of water
Then they'll name their brand
Like Fiji or Perrier
But Madonna, she'll request ten different brands
And worse than that, she'll specify
A volume size popular in Europe
I can't find that shit at Kowalski's
I have to scramble

(4)

My closing question came to mind

As we were about to depart company

Hey, Shopper Guy

What's the most requested item

From your clientele

I expected a thoughtful moment of pondering

But that wasn't the case

Shopper Guy knew his biz, he said . . .

The one thing my clients have in common

They're in the voice game

Voice needs vocal chords

Vocal chords need honey

When possible, I get "Honey Bears"

Honey in a bear is better

Than honey in a jar

At this point I told Shopper Guy

You have served me well

Send my regards to Blue Man Group

BAKING MEMORY #143

The first time I assisted the Frenchman
He was making bark, almond and peppermint
For 30 minutes, I remained silent
Until I got the hang of it
Once comfort was achieved
We discussed Roger Waters
We discussed World Cup Soccer
We discussed the Brittney Griner prisoner swap
One of us thought the trade was fair
One of us didn't
As we built our cases
Younger crew members joined in
Exchanging opinions with smiles and soft voices
Votes weren't cast, but I'd be willing to bet
The general consensus was split down the middle
Later that evening, I considered
Maybe there was no right or wrong
Maybe some things were nothing more
Than a matter of perspective

BAKING MEMORY #144

After greasing the manager
And touring the "Scandal Room"
We had cocktails at the new Whiskey Bar
At the Watergate Hotel
The Tunisian used a quiet voice
Other times he muttered
About Earth, about monuments
During last call
The Tunisian requested a goblet
Filled with liquor foreign to me
I like the word 'goblet'
I wondered if this was determined by
The matter that made up the receptacle
Or the contents that filled it
Then I wondered if a chalice was a goblet
Or cousin to a goblet
After pondering, and further cocktails
It occurred to me
I like the word 'goblet'

BAKING MEMORY #145

On the morning of my 55th birthday
Mother and I sat in a café
She asked what I was ordering
She asked about my new job
How things were going in general
I confessed . . . It occurred to me recently
I was probably alcoholic, but a functional alcoholic
Destroying my life wasn't a goal
I was curious, why did numb feel best
Mother smiled and explained . . .
Drink up kiddo, you won't need to worry
Since you were small, I've known you were a mystic
The whiskey will fade without effort
Because you've reached an age
Where your journey is going to make sense
You won't need to feel numb any longer
The bill was paid, as we went our separate ways
I wondered if what Mother said was true
After a moment, it occurred to me
I couldn't remember an instance
When her instinct wasn't spot-on

BAKING MEMORY #146

If you want to know power
Bake madeleines, know their history
They weren't invented by the French
It was a signature piece
Of a young Polish girl
Sold into French servitude
If you want to know power
Bake madeleines, know their ingredients
Swap out vanilla for orange flower water
Don't be tempted by lavender
Your cakes will taste like a brothel
If you want to know power
Bake madeleines, know your tools
Never use rubber forms
Always use aluminum pans
They shine, they glow
They'll intimidate your mother-in-law
Leaning against the backsplash
On the kitchen counter

BAKING MEMORY #147

She . . . Was a waitress at Al's
And 100 other joints
She . . . Played in an all-girl band
That toured with Adam Ant in Mexico
She . . . Had a clinical fear of rats
She . . . Was an extra on the set of "JAWS"
She . . . Married a rock star we won't name
She . . . Hitchhiked back from a restaurant
Where she worked in Martha's Vineyard
Carly Simon picked her up
I asked what they talked about
She said . . . Nothing, Carly listened to a cassette
I asked . . . Who was Carly listening to
She . . . Rolled her eyes and said
Carly Simon listened to Carly Simon
All the way home

BAKING MEMORY #148

(1)
Days before Christmas
I stood at the loading dock
Waiting for baking supplies
A storm was moving in
Over ten inches of snow was expected
Winds of 30 mph are certain to blow snow
To swirl snow, changing landscape
Creating havoc
It would be normal to worry
About the roads, about my commute
But that seems far off
There's so much left to bake
Within moments of the scheduled time
Beep-Beep-Beep, the produce truck backs in
The driver surfaces
Hops out of his cab and enters the warehouse
I have never seen him before
He determines salutations are in order
Extending his hand, announcing himself
Good morning, I am Marek Tchaikovsky

(2)

With a voice similar to Bela Lugosi's
Marek started a narrative
Explaining a stint in the Polish Armed Forces
It appeared he was partial to tanks
T-72s, T-80s
The M1-A1 and the M2 Bradley
The dialogue surpassed my pay grade
Not wanting to be rude
I smiled and nodded
Until he changed the conversation
To an incident that occurred
With a cable TV man

(3)

Marek said . . .

When my house was robbed, they took our dishes

They stole my children's toys, animals do such things

They took our TV and destroyed our cable

They wrecked it in full, Comcast sent a technician

When he spoke, I knew at once, he was Ukrainian

We talked about many things

We were happy while he worked

When the job was complete, I asked for the bill

The Ukrainian told me

Poland had taken in six million Ukrainian refugees

Giving each one $200

The Ukrainian told me

Your country is saving mine

I see no problem with your cable

There should be no charge

(4)
Marek explained . . .
The Poles have moved out of Northeast
Our security is gone
I can't believe they stole my children's toys
This is a thing only animals do, yes . . .
I nodded before informing
I was half Polish and Irish
The produce driver was delighted and said
This is goodness for you
Your families are from drinking nations
Vodka and Whiskey, these are good choices
Which do you prefer
I responded . . . Whichever you buy me
Marek laughed and asked for my phone number
So we could get drunk next spring
Somewhere Northeast
Without hesitation, I gave him my digits
I hope he calls

BAKING MEMORY #149

(1)

Bobby Vento was tall and handsome
During lulls in production, he danced
Like Bono in the iPod commercial
He pulled me aside to tell me, he was resigning
He wanted more, he wanted better
Months later, I saw him on the news
He had become a supervisor for Comcast
While taking a crew out to secure subscriptions
The building they were working began to smoke
Amidst the flames, amidst the screams
Bobby Vento took control
As residents ran out, he ran in
Scouting the building for trapped pets
Animal souls were saved

(2)

Months later . . .

Bobby Vento entered my office

With a woman whose good looks matched his

She announced they were getting married

As her fiancé went to reunite with the bakers

Bobby Vento's girlfriend hugged me

Telling me, her future husband loved me

I was excited for the wedding

It never happened

Bobby Vento took his life

We had failed to notice his demons

BAKING MEMORY #150

She did pastries
For James Beard Award-winning restaurants
She read my poems
And Barneys of New York catalogs
She showed me how Matisse
Refused to use black to outline objects
She told me she modeled as a child
But after a runway show
All the kids received colorful balloons
Red - Green - Blue and Purple
But she got White
Years later, this led to extensive therapy
She told me, when the world gets ahead of you
Old dogs must learn new tricks
With that said, she hung up her apron
And dedicated her passion
To teaching immigrants how to speak English

BAKING MEMORY #151

A small man with big ideas, a Perry Ellis suit
And eyewear that cost more than my truck
I toured him through the bakery
Stopping in the midst of the facility
A space where the small man explained
His produce company wanted to partner
With butchers and bakers
Who would provide low-quality items
That he would sell at cost
Creating a one-stop shop for food purchasers
I explained I had zero interest
He turned red and burst into a final plea . . .
Are you a fucking idiot, let's cash in
I stepped toward him, the crew circled
All was silent until I explained
Dawg . . . you're out of your lane
He left, we baked, the bread jackals laughed
Referring to me as the fucking idiot

BAKING MEMORY #152

I went to the Guns N' Roses show with Donut Boy
Buckethead with my bread instructor
Baseball card show at the Thunderbird with Minnow
Hyatt chess tournament with Kansas City Bob
Star Trek convention with the waitress
I would have gone to . . .
Game #7 of the 91 World Series with Otto D
But Oven Guy crashed his Harley
Guess who was "on call"
I went, I went and I went
To movies and bars worth discussing
And bars and movies I'll keep mum
So many places, so many people
So many memories, however . . .
Not quite as special as when the chef JD Fratzke
Served me lavender-infused Swedish meatballs
And took me to church downtown

BAKING MEMORY #153

(1)

The powers that be, needed to make a special hire

They brought in a guy from the coast, Mr. Smith

A man who was a dozen years older than me

Many times he saw my future before I did

Mr. Smith loved Jesus and horses

To my dismay . . .

When my life began to skid out of control

He urged me to hop into his car

He drove and drove and drove

To a point where I began to get weirded out

Highway to dirt, dirt to gravel

Gravel across a ranch, up to a barn

(2)
Out of the truck, I stretched, until . . .
Mr. Smith returned with a horse
Walking past me, toward a pasture
When he opened the gate and released the stallion
For an hour we stood silent
For an hour we just stared
While the horse did horse things
Running, galloping and such
But what surprised me most was
How when the horse stood still, I kind of melted
Experiencing a calm foreign to me
On my way home, I confessed to Mr. Smith
I was pretty sure he was going to preach Jesus
Mr. Smith smiled and said . . .
At first I considered it, but once I realized
How messed up you were
It seemed obvious to me
Jesus could wait, you needed horse time

BAKING MEMORY #154

During the 90s, bakeries had an unwritten rule
Queers work the front of the house, not the back
The first exception in St. Paul
Was a young man named Craiger
We worked in a bakery owned by a Pole
Spending PM shifts, baking bread
Craiger was half my size, but moved twice as fast
Most agreed, his talent surpassed impressive
Up till this point, I lived in ignorance
I had met gay men, but I didn't understand them
I was trained, not with words, but innuendo
To dislike them, after befriending Craiger
I questioned why honest men would teach me such things
POOF – The scales were lifted from my eyes
Craiger's fearless joy had Rosa Parks impact
Gandhi impact, on my personal growth
Eventually Craiger left baking and became a postal carrier
Sometimes I see him toting mail in my neighborhood
He always waves, and usually smiles
I wish there was a way for me to express
How grateful I am for all he has given me
But sometimes, the truth makes me shy *wink*

BAKING MEMORY #155

1982 – Little Mikey and I were with dates
At The Festival of Nations
When it was time for me to leave for work
Little Mikey's date, the Dutch woman
Said . . . Stay and eat chips and mayo
I did, after calling in sick, the next day at work
The kingpin left his office. And joined us on the floor
He called everyone together, opened his wallet
And dropped a hundred-dollar bill on the floor
He said . . . One of you left this by not showing up
Yesterday, when your crew needed you
Then he left, returning to his office
The money was still on the floor, hours passed
I was steamed and stormed into the kingpin's office
Muttering . . . That wasn't fair, those guys always call in
And you never chastise them
The kingpin shrugged while reminding me
Those people won't be baking in 20 years
You will, but only if you do better
Then he smiled and told me to fetch his money

BAKING MEMORY #156

Little Sisters of the Poor
Habits and Wimples
Smiles and Mischief
Securing donations
The Polish baker offers a reminder
No priests, no bishops
Our offering is exclusively for the Nuns
We only serve those who serve God
The Nuns blush
Never rebuking this favoritism
The Polish baker places his arm
Around Sister Maria's shoulder
Issuing a final demand . . .
Since I'm giving you these treasures
I want your pardon to skip Mass on Sunday
Sister Maria explains my request is heresy
But when I remind her, I could give the goods
To Lutherans, she hugs me and says . . .
Ok-Ok, you can skip Sunday, if you throw in a cake

BAKING MEMORY #157

For me, I've always picked Paul over John
Hands down, but then I heard
John became a bread baker
Everyone who stopped by his pad
Was sent home with a loaf
I wanted to know more, I reached out to Yoko
Yoko didn't respond, so I contacted May Pang
His mistress May Pang did respond
I started with John questions, with bread questions
May Pang evaded these queries
Instead we discussed Los Angeles
68 Barracudas, our sons, and then eventually
She brought up baguettes and Manhattan
I thought it might be a gateway conversation
Leading back to John and their time together
But that never happened, no matter . . .
Why would I care
I've always picked Paul over John
Hands down

BAKING MEMORY #158

During the holidays, when the clock strikes December
Any baker worth their salt, will pray
For another season of stamina
Somewhere between overwhelmed and numb
The holiday baker understands
They won't see their family, until the ball drops
Announcing New Year's Day
By mid-December, dough hooks bang
Hobart mixers hum
Setting a cadence, practical and magic
Magic enough to erase the external world
By mid-December, your mind spins on ice
Your heart gets lonely
On several occasions I've felt
As if I might fall through the ice
At moments like this, prayer won't help
Conversation is your saving grace
But when there's nobody available
It never hurts to make up conversations
With an absent friend

BAKING MEMORY #159

President Fox
President of Mexico stood 6'4"
On bread crew, a dozen Mexican men
None surpassed 5'10"
I mused on the statistical difference
While running humorous analytics
The bread crew swore at me in Spanish
Ring – Ring the Governor's chef called
Ordering an abundance of dark rye Pullman loaves
For a shindig honoring President Fox
I asked the dozen Mexican bakers
If there was a connection
Between dark rye Pullman loaves and their native land
They shrugged, they advised . . .
Ask the Governor's chef
Just when I was about to, I found out he was fired
Which made me curious, if he was let go
For making a bad bread selection

BAKING MEMORY #160

Vito was an oven man from the Eastside
I was with him when he met his wife
At the Broken Arrow Café
He claimed the sex surpassed expectations
With that said, I endorsed their marriage
He hesitated, until confessing
She's Pentecostal, she speaks in tongues
And raises her hands to the Lord
Vito ended up marrying the Pentecostal
Then I ended up marrying a Russian Jew
Vito and his wife attended our wedding
When the Baptist preacher said Baptist things
Vito's Pentecostal wife worshipped
With a steadfast heart, she raised her hands
And spoke to the Lord in a secret language
Vito blushed, Vito recoiled, until . . .
I broke away from my intended bride
And stood next to the Pentecostal
Raising my hands to the Lord, as well
Vito eventually smiled, while his wife explained
Blessings would surround my wife and I
I didn't disagree

BAKING MEMORY #161

(After Failing Our ICE Audit)
Every day, for 21 years, I ate lunch with Oso
The morning bread mixer
In the employees' break room
Where we combined our food
Onto a single plate
On the final day of production
After setting out our meal
Neither one of us ate
We weren't hungry
Neither one of us could sleep
We were past tired
It had been a 90-hour work week
We just sat together quietly
I didn't know what to say
So I asked . . . You gonna be ok
He nodded before explaining . . .
The biggest mistake I made
Was I got too comfortable
As a Mexican
I should have known better

BAKING MEMORY #162

(1)
Somebody thought it was a good idea
To hire culinary students to work part time
The first two we got
Came from the same technical college
One of the guys was big
Long hair, thick beard
He looked like Bob Seger
The big kid also wore a black biker's jacket
On the back of it was painted
A scripture from the book of Ezra
The kid was quiet, but in so many words
He let us know
It was more than likely
We were on our way to hell
For no reason other than the obvious
The bread jackals refused
To call him by his name
They simply referred to him as Jesus

(2)
The other kid (student)
He was small but supple
And not that it mattered
His looks and intelligence lacked
But for reasons, I don't remember
I do remember, we liked this homely kid
He was a total A-Hole
But he worked hard
And being a gracious asshole
Served as a badge of honor
In the bread jackal community
With that said . . .
We called the kid Satan

(3)
Each day, Monday through Friday
Jesus and Satan reported to work
Around 3:30 p.m.
As they hopped into production
Their added presence was similar to
Puppies being led into a fenced yard
With a dozen Doberman Pinschers
The puppies did their best to isolate
And talk smack about each other
But for the most part
These insecurities . . .
Made the bread crew weary

(4)

On a day, the day turned to night

Jesus and Satan

Were at the other end of the bench

Arguing about moors and bogs

Apparently one of them, or maybe both

Had been to England

Jesus pointed out, moors were dry lands

And bogs were wet

Satan claimed a moor

Could be dry or wet

And basically a moor and a bog

Could be identical

Jesus lost his shit

And poured his temper on Satan

The conflict spilled outside

Onto the sidewalk

(5)

Usually a senior employee imparts wisdom

And does what's in their power to dismantle conflict

But it was summer, it was night

Truth be told, we wanted it to go down

Who would exercise dominion

Jesus or Satan

Gosh it was tense - Gosh it was quiet

As the lot of us mingled around West 7th

I got to be honest

It still makes me feel uneasy in my heart

I found myself rooting for Satan

3-2-1, the fight commenced

Within seconds, Satan popped Jesus

In the jaw, Jesus wept

Instantly Satan dropped his dukes

And shook his head in disgust

As he declared . . .

Fuck this – Fuck all of you, I quit

And I remember, swear to God

As he walked away, I felt nervous

Realizing, I kinda dug Satan

BAKING MEMORY #163

(1)
The Mall of America
Attracts 40 million visitors annually
Outdrawing Walt Disney World
Two to one
Seven Yankee Stadiums can fit inside the Mall
32 Boeing 747s can fit inside the Mall
258 Statue of Libertys could lie inside the Mall
The Mall contains 520 stores
And 50 restaurants
I sold hamburger buns
To one of these restaurants

(2)

I brought in bread samples, mostly buns
I was greeted by the owner
A man who loved himself
As Christ loves the Church
The owner was followed by an entourage
Most of whom seemed to be family members
The group grinned, nervous grins
Before circling me
A chef appeared, a notable man
Flush with credentials
The owner handed the chef some of my buns
While telling him to throw them on the grill
And prepare us some samples

(3)

Halt, I cried, why would you throw perfectly good buns
On a flattop, they looked at me as if I was simple
The chef said . . .
We do it to add flavor
And increase the condiments' durability
This is where I cast my burger bun rebuttal, saying . . .
Tossing the bun on the grill doesn't add flavor
It masks flavor, you know who created the concept
The world's biggest fast food chain
They knew by adding heat
Flavor (or lack of) is replaced by mouth feel
When you buy my buns, by bread world standards
You are pulling a Rolls Royce into the garage
Why would you want to drive a Toyota
The owner became agitated
His Fabio-looking brother announced . . .
Taste testers, somebody find me taste testers

(4)

For a couple of hours
Unsuspecting guinea pigs paraded up to the table
Gorging themselves with burger options
A final tally showed overwhelmingly
Our sampling demographic preferred
Their buns at room temperature
Not grilled
Last time I stopped by this lucrative restaurant
It continued implementing my suggested strategy
But then again, that was years ago
Back when the world was innocent, remember . . .
Locals don't typically go to the Mall of America
That's a pleasure reserved for tourists

BAKING MEMORY #164

Pee Wee returned from the bakery nonplussed
Garbage in his hair, Adidas tread on his face
In addition to scaling bread dough
Pee Wee scaled powder and sold it on the streets
A couple neighborhood thugs gave him a beat down
Said he was a snitch and threw him in the dumpster
Pee Wee was a crackhead, we didn't judge
He was ours, so we pummeled theirs, with fists
Because we were brave enough to avoid guns
Pee Wee made bad choices, spending 10K
He acquired in a settlement, on smoking rocks
With sporting women at the Midway Motel
Pee Wee was in and out of the workhouse
After arranging amorous appointments
In the back of the bread delivery truck
Pee Wee was a crackhead, the crew loved him
He was ours

BAKING MEMORY #165

If the old adage is true, a bakery is only as good as its
    mechanic
For decades we had Tava, he was the best
Like Batman, when peril came our way
The Italian with a tool belt stepped in
Smiling, saving the bread empire
Crawling inside of ovens, or on top of freezers
Friday night, Sunday morning, it didn't matter
We called, Tava answered without exception
One afternoon, while Tava worked on the proof box
I overheard him talking to some Mexican bakers
I mentioned his Spanish was beyond fluent
It seemed so natural, the mechanic explained
My grandparents decided to move from Italy to St. Paul
They booked passage on a ship, when it docked
And they got off, they didn't know the language
It took them a moment to realize they weren't in Minnesota
They were in Brazil . . . Sao Paulo, not St. Paul
While the rest of the family moved to Minnesota
My grandparents stayed in Brazil
As you can imagine, it was harder for them to see us
But they got to watch some great soccer

BAKING MEMORY #166

(1)
The temp was way below zero
I went behind the bakery, to the bread truck
To gather bread racks
Meow – Meow – Meow
Lo and behold, a malnourished kitty
Shaking, freezing, I brought her inside, promptly
Outraged, sickened, staff stared in disbelief
Someone poured milk, someone shared their lunch
Throughout the shift, kitty rebounded
Throughout the shift, the inevitable loomed
The cat couldn't live in the bakery
Someone had to take her home
But who

(2)
You can count on one hand, how many times a year
Production gets stopped, this was one such time
I wasn't a boss, but I found the kitty
So I pitched the following plea . . .
This kitten will become a cat, a covenant with God
Sent here as an opportunity for you
To accept the Almighty's blessings
The Lord had spoken unto me
Issuing the following edict
This precious kitten shall be called "Lucky Duck"
Whoever sees fit to take her home will be shrouded
In eternal abundance, I implemented a dramatic pause
Before asking . . .
Who's going to take this blessing home
Some people mumbled, others looked down
Then like a balloon popping, routine continued
I let it be known . . .
Fuck y'all, blessings unto me and mine
After shaking the dust from my sandals
I took the cat home

(3)
Within the first 48 hours
Lucky Duck pissed 1000 times
Every place except the litter box
This did not bode well with my love interest
Who scooped the kitten up
And took her into a room
For private consultation
As it's been told to me
My love interest said . . .
Lucky Duck, you really suck
Things will have to change
If you piss on my stuff
Or anywhere other than the litter box
You're back on your own
And if you recall, it's a cold, cold world
Lucky Duck flashed a look of defiance
And pranced away
But swear to God, till the day she died
That cat did her business, in the litter
While blessings were bestowed
Unto me and mine

BAKING MEMORY #167

Dear Jesus,
I miss you, I get it, it's my fault
But I gotta tell you, those ambassadors of yours
They don't make it easy
The church tells me to believe in the church
How can I, church is flawed, I am flawed
And even though I have it on good authority
You have special X-Ray glasses
That can see through my soul
I'll confess anyway, I believe in you
And I believe in bread
It's tangible, present every day
Never changing doctrine
Never changing theology
But Jesus, remember, fair is fair
I am willing to repent before the throne
But, it would be my hope
That you would return the favor
And pay a call on me
When things are slow, at the bakery

BAKING MEMORY #168

I hope Chuck liked the wedding cake I baked
Not one of my stronger efforts
But after all, he got married in a bar
326 miles from my house
By a bartender who received religious training
And credentials, online
It was Chuck's second marriage
The bride's too
At 3 a.m. I was halfway home and tired
The highway was empty, I was alone
To prevent sleepiness, I turned on the radio
Alice Cooper was talking about his conversion
He had taken Christ as his personal savior
As he pledged his allegiance, I remembered Mother
How she had said years ago
She was going to add him to her prayer list
I began to wonder if she ever followed through
But then I began to feel foolish
When it occurred to me
Of course she did

BAKING MEMORY #169

(1)
After cherry blossoms
And the National Portrait Gallery
Where it was discovered
The Obama paintings were on loan
To a gallery in Houston
We toiled on, searching through the fray
Of paintings, looking for the portrait
F. Scott Fitzgerald commissioned
An image of himself
An image he couldn't pay for
For reasons unknown
The painting vanished
I left the gallery seeing things important
To everyone but me
I muttered curses, waded through debris
Flagged a cab, and directed it to Martin's Tavern
It was lunch time

(2)

The sun peeped out, diners drifted in

Booth three was open

After greasing the host

My love interest and I were placed in the booth

Where JFK proposed to Jackie O

Sun filled the room, diners drifted in

I raised my ear to the universe

Listening for ghosts

Or displaced dreamers from Camelot

After initial drinks, our server returned

Options were plentiful

But my mind was made up

If the meatloaf was good enough for Nixon . . .

After my date ordered the Ty Cobb salad

She asked to be excused

Before making her way to the powder room

(3)
Alone
I sat in booth three
Wondering
Was I sitting on John's side
Or Jackie's, then it occurred to me
They might have been sitting side by side
The sun reached its zenith
I ordered a Tito's & Tonic

(4)

When my date returned, she said . . .
I love this city, but it's complex
There's something about it, I don't trust
I'm not sure I would want to remain
In the company of cruel men
Then she winked and encouraged me, saying . . .
In your next life, you should come back here
And be President, you're an honest guy
Flattered, I considered my personal obligations
And those to the United States
Before responding . . .
The world needs less truth
And more sourdough

BAKING MEMORY #170

(1)
It was time to sell our Koenig bun popper
Upgrade, expand and build the bread empire
An old man with an accent bought it
With the intention of flipping it
To a bakery in the Caribbean
I asked the old buck if he was Dutch
He wasn't, he was German
I asked about rye bread
I asked about pretzel bread
As we waited for ownership
To return with manuals and documents
Then, with no prompting
The old man described a night
When he went to work
At a bakery in Berlin

(2)

The pastry chef never showed

People were concerned

The pastry chef never missed

When the shift was over, we went outside

Where we were informed, the city was divided

Look Up – Look Down, divided into two

The old man fell silent until he said . . .

It's hard to attach memories

To moments when you were stunned

If they didn't make sense then

Why would they make sense now

I worked with that pastry chef for years

But to be honest, I didn't consider his banishment

It didn't make any sense, what did make sense . . .

I had a bicycle that may have been lost

You'd have to be stunned

To think about a bicycle instead of a person

Don't you think

BAKING MEMORY #171

Because I was uneducated and ignorant
Hatred took a foothold, until . . .
The Quiet Man bought our bakery
At first he exhibited attributes
That clashed with my sensibilities
Soft spoken, sandals, ponytail
Liberal, forgiving and kind
How many times did I roll my eyes
But, when I was hurting
Which was more often than I let on
He didn't talk to me about religion or politics
Instead he mentioned art and baseball
Never once did the Quiet Man
Admonish me, or rebuke my misguided ideas
Instead, he explained paintings
And took me to baseball games
Where we sat in silence, as he filled out box scores
I would have never made it
I would have passed by my happiness
At times I thought he might be an angel
When I found out he shared a birthday
With Elvis and David Bowie, I had my answer

BAKING MEMORY #172

He was owner #2 of 3
At the bakery on West 7th
Bakeries weren't his strong suit, we crashed
But I still valued his loyalty
When I kicked the shit out of Dennis in the cooler
Dennis' lawyer sent photos of his battered client
I felt bad and turned in my resignation
But, Boss-Man told me to stay put
You're an asshole Klecko, I won't deny it
But you're my asshole, get back to work
On a day the sky indicated
Maybe it would rain, maybe it wouldn't
Boss – Man picked me up and drove me
Along with his son, to Chicago
Interleague had become a thing
The Twins were playing the Cubs
At Wrigley Field
Looking back, I don't remember who won
But I do remember how thankful I was
To learn from Boss – Man
That even when business fails
Dignity and loyalty are possible

BAKING MEMORY #173

After 14 hours in front of the oven
Breeze feels good, beer tastes good
Both could be found outside
In the parking lot
Where a dozen bakers circled a cooler
Drinking beer quietly, starting without me
Most of them were half my age
All of them were Mexican
The youngest handed me a Modelo
I opened the can, tilted and swallowed
Noting the satisfaction of the crew
As they faced the breeze
To receive a reward
That would only pay dividends
Until the cooler was empty

BAKING MEMORY #174

The clock struck December
5 a.m. seemed dark as midnight
Outside in the parking lot stood Wanda
Body quaking, squirming in the moment
Her wardrobe didn't handle the elements
The trench coat, knee-high Gestapo boots
Snow blew, body failing, squirming in movement
As I approached, she turned
Deflecting contact, she began to sob
I persisted until she explained . . .
The previous night, her husband pushed her
Down the stairs, after the crash, pain
Amidst the pain, she was escorted
Out of the house, without an opportunity
To gather resources, she slept in her car
The night was everlasting
As I looked for matriarch problem solvers
Wanda reminded me . . .
Things always seem better
When you get to work

BAKING MEMORY #175

I broke off the engagement of marriage
Sold everything I owned, everything
Except six changes of clothes
I was getting out of baking
And moving to Amsterdam
I had a job, passport, one-way ticket
Two nights before I left, the retail manager
Called me into the office and closed the door
She was nine years older, divorced
Wearing Daisy Duke cutoffs
And a fashionable tank top
She stared at me, I gulped
She told me to take off my shirt and turn around
I was scared in a spectacular way
Until she glided fingertips across my back
Then I got scared-scared
As I began to process my fear
She said . . . Go home, you have chicken pox
So much for Holland, within two months
I was married and back to baking

BAKING MEMORY #176

For several years I worked with systems
That focused on taking young men
Recently released from incarceration
And placing them in work environments
Where they could thrive
I grew fond of these men
And had a rooting interest
The only difference between them
And me, is they got caught
A circumstance that manifests
At a higher rate when you're not white
I grew fond of these men
And made it a point
To single them out on the production floor
Where the crew could witness
Me wrapping my arms around them
Hugging them, telling them
I love you, we got this, one tribe
They never squirmed,
Without exception, they smiled
Before announcing . . . Old man is crazy as fuck

BAKING MEMORY #177

Back when . . .
I did push-ups before punching in
Flour was carried in 100# sacks
We worked twelve-hour shifts
Day after day, after . . .
My spirit animal was an Ox
No time to think – lift
No time to want – lift
You can run me through 1000 scenarios
They all reach the same conclusion
Nothing will make a Polish boy
More confident or sexy
Than becoming a bread goon
In a universe that realizes
Duty to strength
Is the equivalent
Of water to wine

BAKING MEMORY #178

She was tall, shapely, had high cheekbones
He was squatty, with a pockmarked face
She was beautiful, he wasn't
I caught a glimpse of them working together
Preparing walleye tacos, side by side
Every time the service door swung open
I caught her smiling, her eyes told the truth
She was enamored, how did this transpire
What could such a perfect specimen
See in a blemished cook, it occurred to me
Hairnets were the common denominator
Both of them wore polypropylene bouffant caps
The ones that look like toilet seat covers
The ones that strip your dignity
The moment you slide it on your skull
Then it occurred to me
Hairnets force us to look past vanity
And into the heart
KABOOM, I finally cracked the code
Once I realized love would be easier to obtain
If hairnets were passed out across the globe
And all of us were brave enough to conform

BAKING MEMORY #179

The luckiest moment of my life
Came after I crashed our bakery
For days I floated, unsure and unwell
The phone rang, it was Lupo
Reaching out and pulling me into the boat
I marveled, he could have passed me by
Already he was established as . . .
The king of Minnesota Baking
How do you say "Thank You" for something like that
You can't, instead you try to be grateful
And feel privileged when he tells you
About Donuts & Danish, and growing up
In New York City, where he heard
The Beatles "Ticket to Ride"
For the first time, in the back of a station wagon
Crossing the Verrazzano Bridge
Or maybe you do try, and say . . .
Thank you John
Thank you very much

BAKING MEMORY #180

(1)
Every year for 10 years
I hosted 50 cooking demos
In the Creative Activities Building
At the Minnesota State Fair
Each year for ten years
I chose a different theme
And found "B" level celebrities
Cookbook authors and journalists
To co- host with me
During the 500 shows
One in particular makes me smile
It was a show where I baked
Irish Car Bomb Bundt Cakes
With a middle-aged media mogul

(2)
The reporter arrived early
The building was closed, lights were off
I took her to my kitchen
We talked by oven light, where I explained . . .
Irish Car Bombs are liquor mixtures
Jameson, Guinness and Bailey's
Poured in equal measure
You can see it oozing through the frosting
As I cut a Bundt wedge, Media Lady swooned
Saying . . . My God it smells like heaven
We were quiet
We ate
She ate more
Her silhouette appeared relaxed

(3)

At a point where she wasn't drunk
But more than buzzed
She told me stories about a woman
About a "friend" who was a baker
A friend she was fond of
Then just like that, Media Lady stiffened
An action indicating an attempt
Of recovering composure
As I collected her plate, I mentioned . . .
There are no secrets in this kitchen
If the woman is your girlfriend
Say it, tell me you love her
I will be happy for you
Media Lady hugged me hard
Thanked me softly
Usually I don't like to be touched
But this time, it felt right

BAKING MEMORY #181

She was there for a paycheck, little else
She was quick to shush us, when . . .
"Walk Like an Egyptian" or . . .
"The Way It Is" came on the radio
One night the power went out
The shift was almost over
We wanted to go home, our boss said . . . No
We sat in the dark, waited, waited, sitting
Waiting in the dark, I became bored
Until she mentioned Bruce Hornsby
Would one day be bigger than Elton John
I guffawed, she rebuked me, asking . . .
Are you a piano expert
I admitted I wasn't, but I let it be known
I was an expert on matters of the heart
She wondered out loud, Why are men so needy
My boyfriend wants me to commit
To loving him forever, hasn't he considered
I am constantly in flux, chances are
He won't be the same person either
Before I had a chance to respond
The boss said . . . Shut up, and sent us on our way

BAKING MEMORY #182

Talk to someone you know
Who has spent an entire career in food service
I'll bet most agree, nobody gets into this
Thinking this would be their first choice
Most people join hospitality because they had to
Maybe they were poor, undereducated or socially awkward
Without connections, or unloved
In the end it doesn't matter
The hospitality industry is made up of
Social misfits from Broken Toy Island
But, in the end, once the worker joins a crew
And their career gains locomotion
Brilliance can shine unique and exotic
Dear Anthony, you didn't leave a note
We failed to recognize your demons
You became rich and famous in an environment
You didn't understand, you stepped out of your circle
Many mornings, before the world wakes up
When I suit up, to head to the bakery
I do my best to remember
In the end, the only thing that matters is the crew
R.I.P. Chef

BAKING MEMORY #183

Tat Bro was the best dough mixer
Known to the Capital City
Young, lean, handsome, shoulder length hair
He looked like a heavy metal front man
During a time, there was a time
Where he began a side hustle
Moving weed, moving powder
Off to jail, do not pass go, do not collect $200
Seven years in a cage, seven days after he was released
He came to the bakery, looking for work
I mentioned, I heard he'd learned electrical
On the state's dime
I reminded him his new skillset would bring more income
But Tat Bro insisted, he needed to spin dough
I did, I let him
After a year, the bath water got warm
Tat Bro was too comfortable
After giving him a hug, I pushed him out of the nest
I think I speak for all the bread jackals
When I say with certainty
Tat Bro, you have made us proud

BAKING MEMORY #184

(1)

I loaded my wares in the Capital City
Before pointing the breadmobile toward Babylon
In route, I recalled a woman, a former bread jackal
Who eventually found salvation in pastry
She was happy, because she was proud
Preparing dessert menus for the Guthrie
A theater that ponied up 125 million dollars
To add a three-stage concept on the river
As ice thawed from my windshield, I decided
I would take time to pay a call
On this woman I just mentioned
Upon arrival, the structure stood impressive
Covered in frost and mechanical blue lighting
The building was locked, I rang a doorbell
Located next to the dumpster
Miracle of miracles, my friend answered

(2)

With delight she toured me

Nobody was there, the morning's crescendo occurred

When I was ushered into the main theater

Wall, carpet, curtain

Rich, regal, red, I felt like I returned to the womb

We sat next to each other in silence

My first thought was

How many times will I see

Dickens' "A Christmas Carol" here

I turned to my friend

Who stared ahead, sinking in contentment

I considered until the obvious became clear

There's nothing you need to think about

Once a moment becomes perfect

BAKING MEMORY #185

(1)
Placed in a conference room
With a Donut Master raised in Duluth
I talked, he talked, I talked
About flying kites in his hometown
With a friend of mine
A budding sourdough baker
I turned quiet, he turned quiet, until I asked . . .
Do you, or did you know Tempe Debe
Donut Master said . . . No
So I continued . . .

(2)

JFK stopped in Duluth

Wanting to one-up the Republicans by being progressive

By starting a narrative about conservation

Enter Tempe Debe, 24 years old

From the Fond du Lac Reservation

She worked downtown as an executive secretary

She guessed which hotel Jack stayed at

She hung around, hung around, hung around

Just as she was about to give up . . . KA-BOOM

A door opened, JFK walked out

Walked toward Tempe, shook her hand

Introduced himself, Tempe was agog

She said he looked perfect

His smile, his hair, his suit

She's never seen a man like that

The President asked questions

Tempe discussed the reservation

Her Chippewa mother, and WW1 veteran father

(3)

Tempe said . . .

It seemed like time stood still

As the President prepared to depart

He told Tempe . . .

After she graduated college

He'd find a place for her

We need people like you

Then he left, as he crossed the street

He turned around and waved goodbye

Eight weeks later

JFK was assassinated in Dallas

(4)

Donut Master grinned, then added . . .

I've never heard that story

Did I tell you my mother baked a cake

For Kennedy during that visit

I was flummoxed, I found that hard to believe

But Donut Master is known for shooting straight

What bakery did she work at . . . I asked

Donut Master grinned and added . . .

She didn't, back in the day

You could do things like that

She talked to someone, who talked to someone

Kennedy got the cake, and get this

On the 50th anniversary of the President's visit

The Kennedy Foundation sent my mom a letter

Thanking her for the cake

No shit . . . said I

No shit . . . said the Donut Master

BAKING MEMORY #186

He came from St. Louis, or was it Kansas City
A tall drink of water, who moved like
A modern Abraham Lincoln
He didn't like anything other than baking
However, occasionally he read
The musings of Joseph Campbell or Stephen King
"It" unnerved him, so he stopped halfway
Somewhere along the line, his fearless nature returned
And he drove to Colorado with his girlfriend
And toured the house where they filmed . . .
"THE SHINING"
In the midst of routine 60-hour workweeks
Most of his free time at home was spent doing . . .
You guessed it, baking
Eventually he moved to Georgia, or was it Florida
During the holidays he sends me sourdough
And holiday breads in the mail
If I had the choice to sanction
Who would tell my stories after I'm gone
It would be this guy
The moment I met him, I knew
I was looking at the future of baking

BAKING MEMORY #187

(1)
Mykonos Ragoff came from Portland
He looked like Keith Richards
Was ten years my senior
Wore a wardrobe that ranged
Between Errol Flynn and Stevie Nicks
He was the oldest student in the baking class
He called me lad, I was his friend
During a period of poverty, when I had to decide
Between feeding kitty or eating kitty
I scrounged up enough money to buy Mykonos
A birthday gift
A carton of Camel straights and a Rolling Stone
With Iggy Pop on the cover
Mykonos was touched, really touched
That's why I was surprised weeks later
When he began keeping distant, I asked..
Bro, what's up, why you in the shell

(2)

Quietly he explained . . .

You've been overbearing lately

Usually that's a sign of insecurity

I'm too old to go there

I responded . . . Fuck You!

He responded . . . Precisely

Days passed, I felt bad

Nights passed, I considered

I would apologize the following day

If I had a chance

I chickened out, the day after that

Before I even saw Mykonos

He was removing a large dough hook

From a Hobart mixer, when Johnny Pittsburgh

Leaned against the "on" button

The mixer was in third gear

KAPOW . . . Mykonos was thrown 20 feet

His arm snapped backwards

Broken in about a million places

I never saw Mykonos again

If I did, I would no longer say . . . Sorry

Instead, I would say . . . Thank You

BAKING MEMORY #188

SEX – SEX – SEX
The Howdy Doody brothers were identical twins
They came from Wisconsin, both were virgins
Billy Baltimore was a salty cuss
Who was the kind of guy, who knew women
Who would help the twins experience sex
For monetary considerations
Billy made the boys pay
For booze, weed and a motel
Once the party commenced, Billy stayed
In the room, watching the amorous deeds
Charging additional fees for sexual upgrades
Billy took Polaroids, the twins bought them
As a memento to remember the loveless evening
They showed these photos at the bakery
Those of us who didn't approve
Of Mr. Baltimore's antics
Encouraged him to shove off, find a new rat hole
Not long after, one of the twins
Chopped off four fingers in the dough-trough
Causing the brothers to reconsider their path
And return to Wisconsin

BAKING MEMORY #189

When George rolled bread sticks he mentioned
He was wearing black fingernail polish
To the Gary Numan concert
Frank announced he saw the Village People
In a club, when he lived in the Bay Area
The crew spelled YMCA with their bodies
Dale mentioned someone puked on him
At a Grateful Dead show
And he used his remaining money on weed
Instead of a replacement shirt
Puppet explained he ran away with the circus
While working Kentucky, he and a carny buddy
Ended up watching Elvis in his prime
Chuckles won an all-expense trip to Milwaukee
For a Pearl Jam show, by cheating a radio station
All these memories, of co-workers' memories
Make me smile, but truth be told . . .
My favorite concert memory was when
Gil got excited, citing details
Of a Bonnie Raitt show, and for no particular reason
The bread jackals burst into laughter
Causing Gil to call them hoodlums, before storming out

BAKING MEMORY #190

(1)
The Halloween blizzard of 91 was legit
It was the first time in my adult life
I participated in a weather calamity
That rivaled those we saw on . . .
"Little House on the Prairie"
Who knew, just two days previous
The Minnesota Twins celebrated
Their World Series victory
With a parade spanning
Minneapolis and St. Paul
About noon the snow started
By 3 p.m. when I had to leave for work
I was afraid to drive, and decided to walk
My commute was 2 ½, maybe 3 miles
Like Pa Ingalls, I made some sappy remark
To my wife, before trudging into uncertainty

(2)

When I arrived at the bakery

Only Pee Wee was there

Boss man decided to shuttle stranded employees

But he got stuck

Tick Tock . . . nobody showed

It was just me and Pee Wee

We broke into the liquor cabinet

Liberated a bottle of rum

We got drunk, we got tired

And went to sleep on pallets of flour

Before Pee Wee passed out, he asked . . .

When you were a kid

Did you ever want to bang your babysitter

(3)

At first I laughed, until I considered
I remember Wendy
For a couple of summers, I saw her
More than my mother
She was beautiful and quiet
When I was with her, she never made me talk
As I got older, I crushed on her hard
She looked like Peggy Lipton on "Mod Squad"
But she had a boyfriend who beat her
Years passed, I didn't see her
Until my 17th birthday
I ran into her at a Kansas concert
She knew I loved her
In ways that were innocent
And ways that weren't
Weeks later she took her life
God – D, the shit you think about
Drunk in a bakery, during a blizzard

BAKING MEMORY #191

(1)
Davey and Dickey weren't friends
But they were friendly, exchanging responsibilities
Running a bakery at a mall
When I first met them
They looked like mountain men
Long hair, grizzly beards
When I left for a new job, they sported
Matching crew cuts and non-prescription eyewear
Somewhere in between, they invited me
To step out to Dickey's car and smoke a joint
Typically, I'm not a weed guy
But these blokes were my bosses
They were cool
I wanted to fit in, impress
Puff – Puff – Puff . . . Talking Heads music
Exhale, more of the same
Puff – Puff – Puff . . . Talking Heads music
Exhale, Dickey turned off the stereo
And explained . . .

(2)
Before work, I stopped at the gas station
I was walking in, and a guy behind me
Was going in too
Usually I don't hold doors open for men
But this guy was an old man
And if I let go of the door
I was worried the old guy would slam into it
I got the feeling he didn't want me to hold it
But I sensed he understood
Our proximity issue, so he allowed it
Davey asked if the old man offered thanks
Dickey answered . . . No actually he didn't
Instead he said . . .
Have a good holiday son . . .
I got to tell you, it made me feel good
Dickey's confession rattled me
Probably because I was toasted
Or maybe I hit a point of maturation
That realizes only honesty
Can break you from confinement

BAKING MEMORY #192

In the walk-in cooler
I heard conversations
That would end political careers
Comments so unholy, all you could do was laugh
In the walk-in cooler
I heard statements
That made closeted skeletons blush
Nuns, cocaine, gerbils, forgiveness
Some things you can't blot out
In the walk-in cooler
I heard ideas
Surpassing a Vegas security clearance
Ideas that scorched eardrums
Most of these statements, most of these statements
Most of these statements were made by
Ass munch trolls, in the walk-in cooler
A place where you'll quickly realize
The human species is flawed

BAKING MEMORY #193

(1)
Sitting in Mitch's Supper Club
I realized I would never advance
In my industry, or life in general
If I didn't add value to my skill set
I was a $12 an hour baker
Who like a normal baseball player
That gets passed around from team to team
Got cycled through all three high schools
Located in District #281
I never graduated, was lightly educated
After a couple of whiskeys, I became brave
I made up my mind
When I was a mid-teen, I read books
But my Mother the Mystic noticed
The authors were exclusively male
She explained the limitations
Of not reading female authors
Or not reading Brenda Ueland
Her book "If You Want To Write"
Taught me to believe in me

(2)
I decided I would write poems
Business articles, essays
But I was uneducated
Fate had it that I catered an event
At the Loft Literary Center
When I told an administrator
I was a poet
They invited me to read
At some February Love Festival
Submitted for your approval
My submission
My first ever submission . . .
MONKEY

(3)
Tattoos and bruises, neither one comes for free
You'll never meet the one who owns you
So why not take a knee
Overtime can kill some time, when you lack family
But all this could be forgotten
If your monkey would only smile at me
The sun was always shining, when I think about my past
Baking with the Poles and Czechs, a predetermined cast
If you wanted a promotion, you simply had to last
But why on earth would anyone wish for that
Many-Many years ago, I never saw a bed
I worked a double shift, and made gas station bread
Sitting in your idiot gauntlet, I didn't think to repent
Another possibility, opportunity never sent
Passing through my hometown, I was rattled by a bum
He set his sights on my opera glasses, and my Tyco drum
Jesus hanging on a cross, he turns and looks at me
Klecko get me out of here, and take me off this tree
I reminded him of salvation's concept
While he screamed blasphemy
But all this would be remembered
If your monkey would only smile at me

(4)
When I finished, many of the poets
Flashed looks of indifference
But when I returned to my table
The chap who sat next to me smiled
And said my piece was esoteric
I smiled
Even though I had no idea
What esoteric meant

BAKING MEMORY #194

(1)
Back in the day, you baked what you baked
Clients could buy it, or go straight to hell
Ring – Ring the phone rang
Production manager fielded the call
Muttering . . . Uh huh, uh huh, yep, gotcha
A fax came with a list of foreign ingredients
Hippie ingredients, healthy ingredients
The type communists bought at co-ops
A recipe landed in the work order basket
The client was the casino
The recipe was handwritten
By George Carlin, who would be performing
The following evening

(2)

I'll admit it, this unexpected mission

Put some pep into the bread jackals' step

Once the production manager left

To gather ingredients

The crew mostly goofed off, laughing

Quoting George Carlin

Helmut took the prize with his maternal voice . . .

Listen young man, I have tried to be

Both a mother and a father to you

(Pause) . . . The voice turned into one

Of a petulant son, saying . . .

Then go fuck yourself

Each jackal howled

The purchase order only called for one loaf

We sent four at no extra charge

George took time to hand write

A thank you card

Classy guy, it was an honor to feed him

BAKING MEMORY #195

Before I passed my prime, I was in my prime
I didn't know it, until I did
I had just finished a media bit
I began puffing my chest, feeling important
La - La - La, look at me, oh so pretty
Ring - Ring, Hello said my wife
She was in a car with a colleague
Another nurse from the oncology center
I thought you were off today, I said
I am, she said, but I have a client
Who wants to die, but she can't, she's afraid
Her beagle doesn't have a home
We found a farm in Wisconsin
It's three hours away
Late that night, nurse-wife arrived home
She said after dropping the dog off
They took pictures and returned to the hospital
The frightened patient lady lost her fear
BAM . . . Just like that, she smiled and died
And here I started off my day feeling important
What a shmuck . . . God Bless, God Bless, God Bless
Oncology Nurses

BAKING MEMORY #196

(1)
Shuemann stepped into production
The crew greeted him
Somebody mentioned he looked frazzled
Henceforth
The legendary rant ensued
Shuemann said . . .

(2)

I don't know why I took a different way to work today
But I did, I took University Avenue
I had to stop at the lights on Snelling
On the bus bench, in front of the bank
Four thugs stood. Looking pissed off
They were staring at me
My windows were rolled down
It was too late to roll them up
If I would have, they would think
I was scared, actually I kinda was
But I didn't want them to know that
I didn't want to look at them
If I would have, they would think I was scared
I had the radio on, "Paint It Black" by the Stones finished
I hoped the next song would evoke power
Something like "Welcome to the Jungle"
Or "Born to Run" might have been enough
To physiologically derail these guys
Of any potential threat

(3)

Instead, fricking Toto came on

That Africa song

I could have died, that fricking falsetto singing . . .

I miss the rains down in Africa

The thugs began to laugh at me

I considered turning the channel

But if I did, they would know I was scared

So I just sat there, and they kept laughing

Those fuckers laughed so hard, they had tears

God Damn It! Toto didn't let up

To be honest

A beat down wouldn't have been the end of the world

But getting your ass kicked

While a keyboard player simulates

A pan flute solo with his synthesizer

That's more than I can endure

BAKING MEMORY #197

Billy Boston was classically trained
At the Culinary Institute of Arts in New York City
Billy Boston lived in Boston
With his mother and some ferrets
Eventually he left his mother
But brought his ferrets to St. Paul
Billy Boston lived upstairs, over the bakery
With a television and his ferrets
He worked 351 days a year
The other 14 he visited Boston and his mother
Billy Boston was nice enough
But it wasn't unusual for him
To time employees when they were in the shitter
When the employee returned
In a heavy Boston accent he'd announce
To everyone and no one in particular
The recent turd time of the employee
Returning to the production floor
Billy Boston was nice enough
I feared he was lonely and invited him to the movies
He declined and continued to love ferrets and time turds

BAKING MEMORY #198

The morning after Philando Castile
Was murdered by a cop
Our office manager alerted us
Philando was a cafeteria worker
Who purchased bread from us
The room fell silent
The office manager continued
Almost every time he ordered
Philando found a way
To say something positive
About his students or life in general
He was a sweet man
I worked with that office manager
For 20 some years
If my memory is correct
That was the only time
I ever heard him call somebody sweet
R.I.P. Philando

BAKING MEMORY #199

(1)
Once upon a time, I started Bread Club
The St. Paul Bread Club
Once a quarter, I opened my commercial space
To people who wanted to learn baking
All kinds of people came
Hippies, Nuns
Republicans, Jews
Journalists and Poets
But my favorite demographic
My favorite people to bake with were . . .
Mothers

(2)
It was a well-attended session
There might have been 51 people, or 67
We were busy, having fun, smiling
Rounding semolina loaves on the bench
A woman my age who was a little boisterous
Asked me to join her, in a place of privacy
Where she could make a proposition
Catholic guilt made me remember
The story of Potiphar's wife
So I said, any deals that will be struck
Will be spoken here, in the light of day
I worked, she rolled her eyes
And hesitated before making her pitch

(3)
My daughter is graduating high school
We are having a huge party
Our family is Italian, I wanted to bake loaves
Italian loaves for 100 people
I have a commercial kitchen, but wouldn't you know
My oven broke
I am in a huge bind
I need the loaves a week from tomorrow
On Sunday, so I was wondering
How much would you charge me
For the use of your equipment

(4)

I explained, for a bunch of reasons
This was a no-win situation for me
I explained she couldn't come close
To affording our bakery and my expertise
The woman remained silent
Looked stunned
Her daughter, who I had yet to meet
Came in the loading dock entrance
From having a cigarette outside
The daughter was beautiful
And in some ways
Reminded me of my daughter
I turned to the mother and said . . .
I will bake your family's bread with you
Right here, next Saturday, 6 a.m. sharp
I will even supply the ingredients
But I have one condition
The mother said she would agree to anything
I pointed at her daughter and said . . .
She needs to be here, she needs to help

(5)
The following Saturday
The mother came, the daughter came
For five hours we baked . . .
Peasant loaves, Ciabatta and Focaccia
After cleaning up, after packing our products
Mother asked how they could repay
I said I would tell them outside
While the kid had a cig
When we got outside, I explained my desire
I told the kid the debt would be wiped out
If she considered quitting smoking
The girl smiled, the mother smiled
The girl asked, what if I consider and keep smoking
That's fair, I said, just consider . . . deal?
Mother hugged me, daughter hugged me
Normally I don't like to be touched
But this time it felt right

BAKING MEMORY #200

The crew almost never went out to lunch
Until a new pastry chef urged us
To join her for pho at a quaint little dive
Deep in the heart of Frogtown
Everything on the menu was tip top
But the pho surpassed special
First it was once a week, then twice
Each time we sat waiting for food
A debate started over a picture on the wall
The picture was a replica of a painting
Much like the one over your grandma's couch
The painting was a seascape
A shoreline with lights bursting through clouds
Like they do in religious postcards
I stated . . . the scene was dawn
The pastry chef said . . . dusk
We argued, we laughed, we argued
One day, Christmas Eve, I entered my office
The seascape was hanging on the wall
I stated . . . dawn, the pastry chef said . . . dusk
The gesture brought immeasurable joy

BAKING MEMORY #201

Topher entered my office
Handed me a time-off request
He wanted May 9th off
So he could recover from the Skinny Puppy show
I rolled my eyes
He grinned a dumb grin, then thanked me
Knowing I would give him the day off
Then he left me alone to consider
The years I worked with his father
The years I worked with his grandfather
Who decades back told me . . .
Kid, you're as strong as Jesse Ventura
Leaning back, I smiled, realizing
I will probably die, broke and battered
I don't have a pension or financial exit strategy
But God-D, I worked in a field
Where I linked arms with families
Three generations deep
I wonder how many people at Wells Fargo
Can say the same

BAKING MEMORY #202

Wherever you find a kitchen
With a healthy amount of Hispanic workers
More often than not
The ritual will begin on Wednesday
When the dishwasher's sister
The oven man's aunt
Or the cook's wife will stop by
Quote the fixed price
And all you have to do is pay up
And select red or green, or both
Friday around lunch time
The woman will return
With bags of tamales, steaming
Smelling like heaven
Any kitchen worth its salt
Has a "Tamale Woman"
A venerable position
Valued greatly, and held in regard
With equal importance
To the person or persons
Who sign the payroll checks

BAKING MEMORY #203

(1)
Years ago, I was contacted
By a German Institute that wanted to know
If I knew how to make German breads
If I could bake German samples
And give a lecture at a big shindig
I reminded them, I was Polish
But truth be told, I was their best option
I baked, researched, baked and prepared
On the event day, I had amassed
A six-foot tower of various rye breads
After dragging them across the venue's threshold
A woman in a red pantsuit
A woman who looked like the performance artist
In "THE BIG LEBOWSKI" issued grave news
Announcing the event coordinator flawed
By double booking the evening's entertainment
The room was packed, I raised my voice . . .
You people got to stop fucking with Polacks
I baked all night, all day, the stage is mine
The Lebowski woman relented
The bread show would go on as scheduled

(2)

As I set up my demo table

My girlfriend (the Russian Jew) whispered . . .

What the fuck

There's a guy in the next room

Next to the bar, sitting at a card table

Selling books about his grandfather

Flying in the Luftwaffe

I stopped, we stared into each other's eyes

Locked in a creepy glance

Until my Russian Jew girlfriend laughed

While relaying in a voice not soft . . .

I should drop your ass right now

But if you go to the bar

And get me a drink

I may reconsider

(3)

When the show started, I announced myself

As the Polish boy

Who was here to teach the Germans

How to make German bread

The show had just started

But most of the audience was half in the bag

They hissed

Which made my girlfriend delighted

To the point where she joined them

In their taunting ways

What's that saying . . .

My enemy's enemy is my friend

As the night rolled on

The Germans were beautiful hosts

They got me drunk, told me stories

About their favorite bakeries in Germany

While plying my girlfriend with pastry

When departure became apparent

They hugged us like family

Urging us to come back anytime

BAKING MEMORY #204

Billy Bama and I got drunk at the Tavern
Where we watched mice scurry
As we discussed born-again folk singers
Which led to James Ellroy novels
Which led to Charles Dickens
I exclaimed, I wrote better than Dickens
Because I had superior inspiration
Billy Bama rolled his eyes
I began to itemize my proof
London versus St. Paul
We both agreed, advantage Klecko
Plum Pudding versus Sourdough
We both agreed, advantage Klecko
We finished with . . .
Orphans versus Bread Jackals
I cast my vote for the bakers
But Billy Bama explained . . .
You got to be high, Orphans are unbeatable
That's why Dickens wins every time
Nobody does orphans better
Until you learn that, you are toast

BAKING MEMORY #205

Marjorie Johnson always wore red
She couldn't be five feet tall
She won more blue ribbons than any living soul
Her oven has thermometers in every corner
Her State Fair entourage dwarfs the Pied Piper's
When Jay Leno flew her to Vegas
To do a bit for "The Tonight Show"
She gave mostly naked showgirls
Muffins to cover their bosoms
During lunch at the Methodist Dining Hall
She mentioned her sensibilities swung right
But once the Republicans wanted to regulate
Women's bodies, it gave her reasons to consider
Once Marjorie turned 100 years young
She stopped counting birthdays
Because . . . Legends live forever

BAKING MEMORY #206

(1)
I don't remember the venue
But I do remember
The baking convention was well attended
I was seated at a table
With my date, with my bread crew
When I looked at the evening's program
I had to laugh, of all the gin joints . . .
Teddy Pento was the featured entertainment
He was conducting hypnotic experiments
Using bakers as guinea pigs
Teddy worked under the name Dr. Matrix
I ran in circles that overlapped his
When I was studying mentalism at Eagle Magic
The stage had ten chairs meant for those
Willing to fall under the spell
And into the trance

(2)
The first eight chairs were occupied
By nondescript volunteers
Chances are they were Lutherans
Bad Billy took chair #9
Bad Billy worked out of Red Wing
In a bakery that he had recently purchased
Gosh, he had charisma
I always admired him
So I took the tenth chair
Once the lights went down
A spotlight bounced off Dr. Matrix
And whichever baker he was hypnotizing
Dr. Matrix instructed . . .
Look into my eyes, you are getting sleepy
When I snap my fingers, blah-blah-blah

(3)

Most of the responses were as expected
Giggling, swearing, one lady got misty
But once the spotlight hit Bad Billy
Everyone in the hall sat up and took notice
As the hypnotist and the baker seemed to battle
Dr. Matrix was almost yelling
Billy turned reddish-purple, veins corded
As he resisted with all his might
The effort was futile, what was he thinking
You can't beat a guy named Dr. Matrix
Just like that, Bad Billy was on his feet
Clucking, flapping imaginary wings
The trance went on and on and on . . .
The audience roared with delight
After the show, my date said . . .
That Bad Billy is wild
I chuckled knowing he'd be twice as bad
Once happy hour started

BAKING MEMORY #207

30 some years ago
After the IRS shut the bakery down
The crew scattered, here and there
Timmy Rapp went back to Michigan
After a month or a year, he called
He was passing through town
He needed a couch, he would only see us at night
He had an agenda, he was safe
Possessing elf-like qualities
Timmy existed on fables and tea
Upon his arrival, upon his first night
He made an excuse about a missed appointment
Therefore joining my clan at the Grandview
To see the movie "HOOK"
The second night he made an excuse
My girlfriend pointed out . . . He's needier than you, lose him
The following morning, I sent Timmy Rapp packing
He said . . . I have nowhere to go, what will I do, I reminded
    him . . .
There's a forest full of elves
Looking for dance partners

BAKING MEMORY #208

Bobby Masterson came from NYC
He was a dough mixer
When the bread jackals found out
He was getting $2 an hour more
Than those with equal responsibility
Division took root
It didn't help that Bobby
Started every sentence with
In New York . . . In New York
Thinking back, not that it matters
He looked like a Bruce Willis antagonist
With physical traits possessed
By those in the Germanic/Albino community
One night, Friday night, he joined the crew
At the casino, he lost his entire paycheck
Within minutes at the blackjack table
He followed winners, asking for money
Security ushered him outside
To the parking lot where he talked shit
Until he got his comeuppance
From the bread jackals
Not that it matters

BAKING MEMORY #209

(1)
It was a thing in Chicago
They threw us in a van
While transporting us across town
Driver guy rattled off statistics
Indicating the neighborhood we entered
Was high on crime and short on hope
Next to an off ramp
In a rundown commercial district
Stood a building, fenced in, barbed wire galore
They called the place "Bee House"
Run by a local woman
And a Romanian beekeeper
The tandem taught those on the fringe
How to harvest honey
How to respect nature
How to love bees

(2)
Those of us taking the tour
Wore beekeeper suits
When I heard the buzzing
I got claustrophobic, panic loomed
A kid in the program, who could have been profiled
As a thug, approached me, explaining . . .
The bees smell fear, lose that shit, now!
Or they'll swarm you good
Getting swarmed isn't something you want
You can trust me on that
Then the kid smiled, and winked at me
Usually I don't like being winked at
But this time, it felt fine

BAKING MEMORY #210

Bagel George was 60-something
Lived with his mother
Most of his nest egg was lost
Batting multiple DUI charges
He was classic St. Paul Irish
Work by day, pub by night
Pub by day, pub by night
His brother was a cop
And a good influence
But, Bagel George loved the pub
To the point of distraction
With that said, I liked him
He read my poetry books
He didn't like them, but he read them
On days off he surfed through thrift stores
Looking for old copies of LIFE magazine
With stories featuring JFK
When the plague came, he refused the shot
Landing him in the hospital for three months
I haven't seen him since

BAKING MEMORY #211

3 a.m.
The baker loads 500#s of bread
Into a car, with the assurance
He will reach the Great Lakes before dawn
To build a sourdough tribute
A temple on the shoreline
A gesture to remind himself
It isn't prudent to run
With the hare and the hounds
All those years, all those years, wasted
Honoring critics and consumers
All those years and not so much
As a widow's mite offered
To the universe with gratitude
Once the temple is complete
The baker steps back, waves crash
A master of sound and rhythm
In the darkness, in the sand
The sun pops up, leaving the baker to wonder
Is this the end, or a new beginning

THE END

ABOUT THE AUTHOR

On the rare occasions when Klecko is not in the bakery, you can find him at the Grandview Theater watching "Oppenheimer," reading Sinclair Lewis or at the Owl Bar in Balto having cocktails with his sister.